JOE ROGALY

Parliament for the People

A handbook of electoral reform

TEMPLE SMITH·LONDON

First published in Great Britain 1976
by Maurice Temple Smith Ltd
37 Great Russell Street, London WC1
© 1976 JOE ROGALY
ISBN 0 85117 1001 (cased) 0 85117 0994 (paperback)
Photoset by Red Lion Setters, Holborn, London
Printed in Great Britain by
Billing & Sons Ltd, Guildford and London

to my parents

Contents

Introduction:
Power to Parliament

This report is offered as a manifesto for militant democrats. Our dear old British constitution has become just that: it costs us very dear, and it is very, very old. It has never worked for long without requiring some important alteration in some of its parts, as in the voting reforms of 1832, 1867, 1885, 1918 and 1948. Now it needs a complete overhaul. It may have worked, more or less, in times when it did not matter much whether what the people wanted was what the people got, but it does not work today. It does not give us representative government. Parliament has been devalued. The country is in a mess. If it is to be rescued, democrats must take charge — or others will.

The word 'democrats' is not used lightly. This is not a manifesto for those who just for the moment think of themselves as 'moderates' or 'coalitionists' or 'representatives of the sane centre'. A change to a fairer system of voting may very well put just such people into the government in the first election under the new rules, but that would only be because most voters wanted an administration of that kind. If it turned out, now or later, that most voters wanted a collectivist government according to the principles of Chairman Mao, or, conversely, a 'business government' according to the principles of Adam Smith — well then, that is what a democratic British constitution would provide. This is a fundamental principle of this manifesto.

Whenever a set of new political rules is proposed everyone naturally asks, 'how will that affect my party?' If the answer is, 'it will help them to win' you then hear, 'excellent, what a democratic scheme!' But if the reply is, 'it will probably keep you in opposition until you can attract more support', the response will be, 'unfair, unjust and unworkable — we cannot have that — it does not provide strong government — the people will not accept it — nobody will understand it — it is too complicated — it would be very costly — it would bring on more rain' — and so on. This need not be pure cynicism. A good socialist will be convinced that the way to improve the

world is to govern according to the principles of socialism. If
that means accepting rules that give the party a chance to do
so against the wishes of seven or eight out of ten of the voters it
is to be deprecated, but the passionate Socialist will feel certain
that greater good would be done by having his or her party
form the Cabinet even on such a doubtful foundation.
Likewise a Conservative, or a Liberal, or a simple believer in
the defence of the individual against the state, may come to
the conclusion that it is better for the country to be governed
under unfair rules that give his or her party a majority of seats
when it has a minority of votes than take a chance on the
victory of other people who are surely less aware of what is
right for the country than a Conservative or Liberal
government would be.

What these people are saying, if they could just stop and
think about it for a moment, is 'I know better than a majority
of my countrymen what is good for them, and they will have to
take it'. Whatever this may be, it is not the voice of a true
democrat.

Nor is it the voice of a genuinely practical politician. There
was a time when incoming governments did not set about
automatically reversing everything their predecessors had
done. Until 1964, activists inside the Labour Party who
opposed the mixed economy could be kept more or less under
control. After 1948 the Conservatives more or less learned to
live with the National Health Service. Nowadays the overthrow
of the most prominent works of the previous regime seems to
be automatic. The cry 'we will repeal that' is the common
slogan of both major parties when in opposition. For the
ordinary British citizen anxious to go about his business the
confusion is worsened when it is realised that much of this
building-up and tearing-down is pure sham; on the central
issue of how to manage our domestic affairs both Labour and
Conservative governments have discovered that there is a limit
to the amount of unpalatable medicine that can be forced
down the public's throat without its consent. Mr Heath's
somersault of midsummer 1972 was matched by Mr Wilson's
somersault of midsummer 1975. The U-turn has become a
normal feature of British administrations.

All this means that minority-party dreams of imposing one
set of values or another on British society are in the short run

damaging, and in the long run frustrating. A government can get away with it in the first year or two after taking office, but not, it seems, for much longer than that. This is hardly surprising, since modern British governments are not only unrepresentative, they are generally seen to be unrepresentative. The lesson is inescapable: Conservatives who hope for a return to more laissez-faire economic policies have a choice between a brief flirtation with such a counter-revolution, or a long-lasting marriage, with all the compromises that that implies. Equally, Labour can fail, fail and fail again to impose full-scale socialism on an unwilling Britain, or it can try for something more durable by accepting that the only real change in the shape of society is the one that at the minimum commands the acquiescence of most of the people, and at best enjoys their whole-hearted consent.

Suspicious ideologists on either side of the main dividing line will deride this as the argument of wishy-washy supporters of the 'soggy centre', while those who fancy middle-of-the-road policies may say that since it seems to give a good chance for social democrats it is a fine idea. All this, it must be repeated, is beside the point. A Conservative government under Mrs Thatcher might try to turn Britain to the right again, and, if that was what a majority of the people wanted, good luck to it. A Labour government under, say, Mr Wedgwood Benn could move its own leftwards way, and if the votes proved that that was the people's will, then good luck to Prime Minister Benn. Or, if what the people happen to want is the soggy centre, then that is what they must have. Who knows, it might not turn out to be quite so soggy after all, especially if the voting system produced a Parliament that everyone could see genuinely reflected the will of the electorate.

Such a government might have to be a coalition. If so it would at least be ruled by *open* coalition, in which parties representing the various strands of opinion could be seen by their electors to be defending, or betraying, the values they held dear. This would be better than the submerged coalitions we now get under the labels 'Conservative' or 'Labour'. Such governments invariably represent fewer than half the voters, and the party factions do their secret deals behind the scenes, leaving the voters in ignorance and therefore relatively defenceless. An open coalition, on the other hand, would almost invariably contain within the government representatives of more than half the voters. If principles were betrayed in order to form the coalition the voters would see who was to blame. They would be in a position to vote the offending rascals out next time. In fact some parties likely to form coalitions in countries where there is fair voting have in recent years made it a practice to state clearly before the election is held just what their terms for joining a government afterwards would be. This gives voters a better chance of choosing a government than our present system of submerged coalitions which we mistakenly call two-party democracy.

This book explains how blind politicians have been taking our country over, each party in turn, each in the innocent belief that what was being done was made sacrosanct by the blessing of the people, and each tragically wrong. It proposes an important change in our system of voting, which is the least democratic of all voting systems in Western Europe. Only four of the twenty leading democracies in the world vote the way we do: ourselves and New Zealand, which could both do with a change; Canada, whose division into provinces makes it not strictly comparable; and the United States, whose totally different federal constitution, with its written rules, its strict separation of the power of the President from the powers of Congress, and its independent Supreme Court, makes it quite different from us. All the rest, including France, Australia and Japan, which run second-best systems, have voting rules which give people a fairer choice. Successful countries like Sweden, Switzerland, Holland, Denmark and West Germany enjoy the luxury — in a British democrat's eyes — of Parliaments whose members more exactly reflect the opinions of the people they represent.

There is no mystery about the various systems of voting that most other democracies use, or about the many other options that have been proposed over the years. It is simply a question of looking them up, and noting how other, fairer, systems are working in practice. Part Two of this book sets out to do this from the point of view of the militant British democrat. But first it should be acknowledged that a change in our electoral system would not in itself cure all Britain's constitutional or other problems. The way we vote does produce startling results, as the first three chapters will show, but it would be overstating the case to assert that if a better system of voting had been in operation since 1945 Britain would not now be the poor man of Europe, with a sick economy, a confused society, and a general sense of foreboding about the future. It *might* have had wiser, more popular government, and to that extent it might have been better off, but there are so many other causes of our present malaise that a bad and increasingly unworkable voting system cannot be singled out as the only one.

It would thus be false to assert that a change to a new system would be, as Mr Len Murray, the leader of the Trades Union Congress, has said in another context, 'the greatest thing since sliced bread'. It would provide an opportunity for an escape from the stale, unrepresentative and divisive government from which we now suffer, but if our society is not ready or willing to grasp that opportunity a change in the rules of voting will not make much immediate difference. West Germany has become one of the most stable, progressive, and democratic modern European countries under its strictly proportional system, but another, quite different, form of proportional representation has not been sufficient to save Italy from a political and economic fate that makes everyone in Britain say 'it's worse in Italy' and everyone in Italy say 'it's worse in Britain'.

A third qualification of the argument that electoral reform is of the utmost importance if the British way of life is to be saved, is that other changes in the way our governments go about their business would have to follow. The political parties and the civil servants have long been accustomed to the idea that what must be avoided above all is a defeat for a government on a vote by MPs in the House of Commons. The average voter probably feels less strongly about this, but anyone trained in Westminster or Whitehall would have to unlearn a great deal of what has been learned under the present rules. It should no longer be regarded as a catastrophe if shifting coalitions in Parliament alter aspects of this or that law, or even decline to pass whole new laws, or introduce laws of their own. The method of bringing a government down would best be a formal vote of no confidence taken for just that purpose. For the rest of the time Cabinets — and consequently Whitehall and the Civil Service — would have to accustom themselves to the strange (to them) notion that what happens in Parliament is very important indeed, and that rule by getting an interdepartmental committee to put an idea across to the Minister, who then gets Cabinet approval and automatic passage from an inbuilt majority in the Commons, would no longer be quite so easy. Of course governments could not last if they could not get most of their programmes through, but the balance of power between Cabinet and Parliament would be shifted in favour of Parliament. Indirect rule by unparliamentary and unrepresentative outside bodies like the Trades Union Congress, or business interests, would be replaced by government by the chosen representatives of all the people.

Many other changes would be necessary. If Members of Parliament were to become important figures in the land, representing the views of the people in a serious way, the secrecy of Whitehall would become even more difficult to defend. It serves the purposes of inner-clique government, but not of government by Parliament restored. Parliamentary committees would become far more powerful, and more able defenders of the electorate's wishes. In these circumstances the House of Lords would best be replaced by an elected Senate; once democratic reform begins you never know where it might end! For the restoration of the functions of Parliament need not be an end to the restructuring of our constitution. Several other ideas have their attractions at first sight: regional assemblies in England as well as Wales, Northern Ireland and Scotland; a formally-stated written Bill of Rights; even fixed-term dates for elections, thus ending the practice whereby Prime Ministers can call elections when it suits them rather than the people. If a government was dismissed by the Commons in mid-term the Queen could ask for someone else to form another, or in special circumstances there could be a dissolution.

Each of these proposals would require a dissertation in itself, and this is not the place to assess the merits of such possible later steps in the march of militant democrats. The simple need at this stage is to acknowledge that other aspects of constitutional reform are likely to present themselves as Britain moves out of its present stage of near-ungovernability. Electoral reform is the best immediate hope for democrats. It may not be the only reform necessary. It would be an important first step.

PART ONE

The games politicians play

1 Russian roulette

Britain's system of choosing governments is breaking down. It is unfair. It does not produce Parliaments or policies that reflect the will of the people as a whole. It no longer guarantees the emergence of strong, widely-respected Cabinets. It is damaging our democracy, making a nation that is difficult to govern almost impossible to govern. The system is out of tune with the times.

In October 1974 the Labour Party won 39.3 per cent, or fewer than four out of ten, of the votes cast. This gave it enough seats in Parliament, and what it chose to regard as a people's 'mandate', to form a government. Yet its basis of proven popular support was even less than its share of the votes actually marked and folded and stuffed into ballot boxes seemed to show. Taking into account everybody who could vote if they wanted to, including those who stayed at home, Labour's share worked out at 28.6 per cent — well below three out of ten of all the people aged over eighteen, excluding criminals, lunatics, and peers. It might be said that those who did not vote were expressing an opinion of some kind: that they were satisfied with things as they were, perhaps, or that they did not like any of the candidates on offer, or that since they were in safe seats it seemed pointless to take the trouble to vote. Whatever the reason the fact remains the same: less than twenty-nine out of every hundred voters took the trouble to mark an X by the names of candidates representing the party that eventually formed the government. If we saw in the newspapers that in some foreign country seven or more out of ten of the people were either against their government or unwilling to express support for it we would call that country one of several unpleasant names. In no way could it be called a democracy. If we were then informed that in this hypothetical non-democratic country the ruling faction imposed policies supported by fewer than, say, a fifth of the people we might wonder how that country could be governed at all.

The sad truth is that the policies that the Labour

government tried to carry out between March 1974 and June 1975 were asked for by an even smaller proportion of the people than its fractional minority of the possible vote (29.3 per cent in February, 28.6 per cent in October) might indicate. These were politicians' policies, arranged as a result of debate or argument between small groups inside the party, with the opinions of the Trades Union Congress almost always paramount. Some of them may have been good policies, and some of them may have been bad, but it could not honestly be said that these were the policies demanded, or even assented to, by more than a small fraction of the people. This is not a party-political argument. The Conservative government that was elected in 1970 was supported at the polls by just one-third of the registered voters. It soon became clear that some of its policies, worked out by a few men and women inside the party during its spell of opposition, were unpopular. Half-way through its term of office that Tory government reversed some of its earlier policies in an effort to win back support from the voters, just as after midsummer 1975 the Labour Government moved away from what its party had ordained towards what a greater number of people might find acceptable. In both cases it was the pressure of events that forced the governments to turn away from much of what had been worked out by the political parties that supported them. In neither case did a majority of the voters have any direct say in the matter.

It is true that according to our present illogical rules there might have been some justification for trying to pretend that Labour 'won' the election of October 1974, since the other parties fared worse. The Conservatives attracted only 10.5 million votes, a million fewer than Labour and less than at any time since 1945. The Liberals' vote of some 5.3 million was about 700,000 down on their post-war record of six million won half a year earlier. Thus it could be said that with its 11.5 million votes the Labour Party had the biggest pile of ballot papers behind it, even though it was nothing like as big as those of the other parties put together.

There was not even that kind of simple-minded justification for claiming that Labour won the February 1974 election. For on that occasion the Conservatives ended up nearly a quarter of a million votes ahead of the Labour Party — 11,872,180 for the party then led by Mr Edward Heath, to 11,646,391 for Mr

Harold Wilson's party — yet it was Mr Wilson who, after waiting a long weekend while Mr Heath made up his mind to resign, went to the Palace to hear the Queen ask him to form a government. Of course it would have been just as absurd to claim that the Tories had won as it was to claim that Labour won either of the general elections of 1974. In February Mr Heath's party was given the X of approval by just under 30 per cent of those eligible to vote and only 37.8 per cent of those who in fact did vote. The Conservatives' vote was 1.3 million down when compared with their 1970 victory total. Quite plainly Mr Heath's government was thrown out. But was it so plain that Mr Wilson's team, with even less popular support behind it, had been given the people's trust?

If it is asked, who then *should* have formed the government in February 1974? — the answer is that under the existing rules Mr Wilson was quite within his rights to take office. By the pure accident that is the outstanding feature of the British electoral system, the 11.6 million voters who chose Labour in February 1974 sent 301 MPs to Parliament, making Mr Wilson's the largest party in the House of Commons. The Conservatives won more votes (11.8 million) but our fruit-machine politics gave them fewer seats — 297 — in Westminster. Now even 301 seats is not enough to form an overall majority in the House of Commons (you need 318 MPs for that) but the convention is that the Queen sends for the leader of the largest party. In February 1974 that turned out to be Mr Wilson. In a proper democracy, in which politics is not seen as a game of cricket with each team taking it in turns to have an innings, the Labour leader might have invited members of other parties to join his minority government. In Britain in 1974 this was absolutely taboo, as Mr Heath discovered when he tried to stay in office by doing a deal with the Liberal Party.

Unwanted MPs
In October the Labour Party won even fewer votes than in February (although more than the Conservatives), but the luck of the draw gave it eighteen more MPs, thus turning it into what could technically be called a 'majority' government. The phrase 'the luck of the draw' means just that. In a British election the candidate who wins is the one who is fortunate

enough to attract the most votes. This is quite different from saying that a majority of the people in any one constituency favour that candidate. If there are three candidates standing — say, Labour, Liberal and Conservative — then in theory it would be possible for one of them to win with one-third plus one of the votes cast, assuming that the votes were spread almost equally between the three of them. With four candidates in the race — one from each of the three national parties plus, say, a Scottish Nationalist — the winner needs only one-quarter plus one of the votes cast to be declared Member of Parliament for that constituency.

This is more than a theory. It happens in practice. For example, one M.L. Brotherton sits as Conservative MP for Louth on the basis of 19,819 votes cast for him, and 31,686 votes cast against him. The breakdown, in the October 1974 election, was: Conservative 38.5 per cent, Labour 32.9 per cent, Liberal 28.6 per cent. As a proportion of all those entitled to vote, including stay-at-homes, the proven support for this 'representative' of Louth is less than three out of ten.

Nor is this an isolated example, or the most extreme that could be chosen. The Labour MP for Caithness and Sutherland, R.A.R. MacLennan, 'won' in October 1974 with 35.3 per cent of the votes cast. The Liberal member for Inverness, D.R. Johnston, was sent to Westminster after that same election on the basis of the support of 32.4 per cent of those who voted in his constituency. And in Dumbartonshire East, Mrs M.A. Bain was 'elected' to represent the Scottish Nationalist Party and her constituency by 15,551 votes — a whole 22 more than the 15,529 votes won by her Conservative opponent, and 429 votes more than the 15,122 votes won by the Labour candidate. In proportion the split was: Scottish Nationalist 31.2 per cent, Conservative 31.2 per cent, Labour 30.3 per cent and a trailing Liberal with 7.3 per cent. Counting those who did not turn up to vote, three-quarters of the people of Dumbartonshire East did *not* show that they wanted Mrs Bain as their MP. Yet it was Mrs Bain they were given — by our lucky-number electoral system.

None of this is meant as an objection to the winning of places in Parliament by Messrs Brotherton, MacLennan, Johnston and Bain; each one of them may well be an excellent guardian of the interests of his or her constituents. They would however be much better representatives if they had been elected by a more logical process, one that left no room for doubt about whether or not most of their constituents wanted them to be in Parliament in the first place.

There are many Brothertons, MacLennans, Johnstons and Bains in the House of Commons. In October 1974 no fewer than 380 of the 635 seats were won on a minority vote — that is, 380 MPs were sent to Westminster with more votes cast against them than for them. This was not quite so bad as in February of the same year, when the figure was a record 408, but it is still worse than in most other election years (in 1964 it was 232, in 1951, 69) and it is further evidence that the notion that we have a two-party system with each of the parties beloved by just about half the voters is becoming demonstrably more absurd with every year that passes. Yet this is the method of voting that is held up as giving the individual Member of Parliament a distinctive, intimate link with his or her constituents!

Unproportional representation

The luck of the draw works in another peculiar way. It so happens that in many safe seats, mainly in cities, there are heavy concentrations of Labour voters, while in safe seats in areas like the Home Counties many Tories are to be found, some of them living in neat suburban houses. The effect of this is that a constituency like Stepney and Popular, to take one of the more striking examples, will usually provide almost any Labour Party candidate with about 75 or 80 per cent of the votes cast in any election, while in, say, Croydon South the Conservatives can usually look forward to at least 55 or 60 per cent, or possibly more, in a straight two-party fight. Piling up the votes in some constituencies in this way turns the national result into a throw of the dice. There is rarely very much sense to be made of the relationship between the votes cast by the electorate as a whole and the numbers sent to Parliament. Professional students of elections have a rule-of-thumb called the 'cube law' that is supposed to explain this, but it does not work very well when the two-party system breaks down, as is happening today. It is because of this uneven distribution of votes that a party can win a majority of seats even though it has fewer votes than the 'losing' party. The unfairness of the system is made especially clear when the number of votes cast for each party is divided by the number of MPs representing that party. In October 1974, on the basis of that test, it took:

35,915 voters to elect one Labour MP,
37,771 voters to elect one Tory MP,
40,777 voters to elect one United Ulster Unionist MP,
55,440 voters to elect one Plaid Cymru MP,
76,328 voters to elect one Scottish Nationalist MP and
411,288 voters to elect one Liberal MP

If the rules had been fairer and more logical the results of both 1974 elections would probably have been different. Instead of the hidden coalition of the left and right wings of the Labour Party (with a non-Parliamentary force, the Trades Union Congress, influencing its every move), there might have been an open coalition, openly arranged. It might have been led by the Conservative, Labour or Liberal Party, according to how the voters decided and how the parties operated the system. Instead of a weak and divided Conservative opposition, itself a hidden coalition, and four or five other opposition parties, there might have been a strong publicly-sealed compact of opinion of the anti-government benches. The politicians' unwritten coalition that kept Mr Wilson in power after his government's U-turn of midsummer 1975 (because the Conservatives feared that if they brought the government down they might themselves be defeated or split asunder) might have been influenced by the votes of the people in a fresh election. Or it could be that no such wheeling and dealing would have been necessary in June-July 1975. If the people had voted under a new fair-shares system in October 1974 in the same way as they in fact did vote under our system of winner-takes-all, then the results might have been affected as shown in the table opposite. This makes it easy to see why the two largest parties shy away from any serious discussion of electoral reform. Yet it would be a mistake to regard such figures as much more than an indication of how unfair the present system can be. A more sophisticated table can be found on page 329 of *The British General Election of February 1974* by David Butler and Dennis Kavanagh. Calculated by the election specialist Michael Steed, it shows the different results that might be expected from various systems of proportional representation. In each case the figures differ by little more than a handful of seats from those produced by the crude arithmetic below.

party	share of votes %	more seats won	fair share of seats	difference
Labour	39.3	319	250	−69
Conservative	35.8	277	227	−50
Liberal	18.3	13	116	+103
Scottish Nationalist	2.9	11	18	+7
United Ulster Unionist	1.4	10	9	−1
Plaid Cymru	0.6	3	4	+1
Others	1.7	2	11	+9

All 'might-have-been' tables of this kind suffer from the fact that nobody can tell precisely how much cunning there is in the British electorate. If the rules were changed, some people who vote rarely or never might decide that a trip to the polling station would be worthwhile after all. Others might vote quite differently from the way they do now. There might be even more Liberals sent to Parliament than the crude arithmetic suggests, on the ground that the Liberal Party would at last stand a chance of once more leading a government; or those for whom Liberal was a protest vote might return to the Labour or Conservative parties knowing that at least they had a chance to pick both the wing of the party they preferred and the type of MP they wanted to represent that wing; or quite new party combinations might arise and voters might find themselves choosing between Conservatives, Liberals, Social Democrats, and true Socialists in a manner that is probably better suited to the mood of Britain in the late 1970s than the party structure that owes so much to the experiences of half a century ago.

The good reason for a change to a fairer system of voting is that it could lead to a more genuinely representative and democratic form of government. The bad reason would be that such and such a change would be calculated to produce such and such a result, favourable to one political group or another depending at least in part upon the electoral method chosen. There are many systems to choose from, and it would be a tragedy if protracted arguments about which is best (or which suited party managers best) led to a stalemate and no reform at all. Yet it must be said that while just about any change would be better than keeping the system we have, the most sensitive mechanism of them all would be the single transferable vote, a system that gives everyone a choice between several candidates and a chance to mark a ballot paper in order of preference, 1-2-3-4. (It is assumed at the outset that our expensively-educated post-war generation has enough wit to do better than just scribble an X against the name chosen by the local party committee.) This system, which could with advantage be re-christened the 'super-vote' (see Chapter 9) has been fiddled by successive governments in Ireland, the major country in which it has been used. As practised over there it is less fair than it could be, although it remains a whole lot better than the great British gamble. Militant British democrats could learn from Ireland's mistakes (see Chapter 10), or they could choose the almost equally attractive 'double-vote' system, used in West Germany. This is scrupulously fair to all save the very smallest fringe group political parties, but it is not anything like so sensitive to the idiosyncracies of the individual voter as the super-vote (see Chapter 8).

In both Ireland and West Germany the trend over the years has been towards two-party government, with fourth and fifth parties falling by the wayside while the third party has either not made much headway or suffered steadily dwindling support. Nobody can predict exactly what would happen under fair voting in Britain; it would be a unique and refreshing experience for us all. But there seems little doubt that at least in the early years no party would win an overall majority in the revitalised Parliament. There would probably have to be a coalition of some sort, although it is quite possible for the largest party to form an administration on the basis of a minority of votes in the Commons — the important difference being that such a government would be obliged to pursue policies broadly acceptable to some members of other parties as well as its own. Any coalition would probably be led by Labour or the Conservatives, but it could be made up of a combination of left-wing Conservatives, mainstream Liberals and Labour moderates (perm. any two out of three), and there might be some general changing-about as a result. Is this so startling? A Labour Prime Minister relied on precisely that combination of Parliamentary forces in promoting his policies on British entry into the European Common Market, wage control, and defence. This was an unwritten, unspoken, politicians' coalition of 1975; fair voting could have made it a voters'-choice combination. The important fact about any such government — assuming that that was the people's choice — would not be its social democratic face, but rather the wide, proven level of popular support for its policies. By definition it would have at least half the voters behind it; in practice its poll would usually be greater than that. In subsequent elections the victors might be individual left, right or centre parties or groups of parties. This should not trouble honest democrats of any party. What matters is that governments should broadly reflect the will of most of the people most of the time.

The decline of the two-party system

It might be objected that all the argument so far has been based on the two elections in 1974; these could have been freak results. It is quite true that the situation has been getting worse over the past decade and that judged by 1974 standards there might be an apparent improvement when the results of the next general election are counted. On the other hand the system has produced unfair results for many years; the only real difference about 1974 was that the unfairness was so gross that people began to take notice. For like so much else in our political life the way we choose Parliaments could almost have been designed by hostile forces, whose single purpose was to divide the British people, set them at one another's throats, and so weaken the nation. The present system, with firmly established national parties trying their luck in single-member constituencies, was introduced in 1885; it is a curious coincidence that the period since the turn of the century has been one of almost continuous economic decline (relative to our main competitors) and increasing internal instability. The main periods of unity and 'greatness' have been in wartime, when the effects of childish winner-takes-all voting have been temporarily set aside in Parliament, in the interest of fighting the common enemy.

There have been twenty-five general elections since 1885. In only five of these — 1886, 1900, 1906, 1931 and 1935 was the

result a government that could claim that it had the support of
more than half the voters, wartime coalitions aside. (In another
five cases the resulting government rested on less than four out
of ten of the votes cast.) In 1951, for example, the Labour Party
won over 200,000 more votes• than the Conservatives, but
because of the Russian roulette that we in Britain use as a
voting system, the Tories 'won' the election: the spin of the
wheel gave them 321 seats in Parliament to Labour's 295. This
was just as indefensible then as it was when Labour 'won' on
the lower total of votes twenty-three years later.

The two large parties have not complained, however,
because what the leader of each of them wants is a chance to
enjoy the almost unique amount of power that a British Cabinet
can wield while it is taking its 'turn' in office. In Britain there is
little to stop a determined Cabinet with a Parliamentary
majority behind it from passing whatever laws it pleases,
although persuading the people to accept an unpopular law is
another matter. The Opposition can make a fuss in the House
of Commons, but that is all. The House of Lords, which is
elected by no one, can amend the bills sent up to it, but back
in the House of Commons the Cabinet's voting troops can
overrule the amendments. There is no written constitution, no
balancing Bill of Rights, no countervailing power kept firmly
in the control of the courts. The party that happens to control
a majority of the seats in Parliament is supreme, and the men
who rule the party that our wheel-of-chance elections happen
to put in as the 'government' are less troubled by constitutional
checks and balances than their counterparts in any country in
Western Europe, with the possible exception of France.

In earlier times, when most politicians could usually be
relied upon to observe the unspoken but widely recognised
rules of gentlemanly behaviour that made this system just
tolerable, it could be said that any change in our 'strong
Cabinet' form of government might be for the worse. In
today's atmosphere, when old-world courtesy is hard to
discern, and respect for what were formerly taken for granted
as the constitutional proprieties is on the wane, an informal
constitution, whose rules are simply 'understood' by those who
operate it, is almost impossible to work. It is hardly surprising,
therefore, that people are becoming more and more
contemptuous of our major party politicians. In 1945, the year

of the Labour Party's most cherished remembrance, some 12 million people turned out to vote for Mr Attlee and his colleagues. The party's vote increased in the two following elections, reaching a peak of 13.9 million in 1951 (an election it would have won if the rules had been fair). But that was the end of the great crusade. For with the single exception of 1966 Labour's vote has fallen in every election since then. In October 1974 it was down to 11.5 million — half-a-million less than it was in 1945! During that time the population grew, eighteen-year-olds were given the vote, and the number of people on the electoral roll increased by nearly seven million: from 33.2 million in 1945 to 40 million in 1974. Seven million more voters — and yet Labour fell back to where it was thirty years previously.

Again, this is not a mere party-political point. The Conservative performance is just as bad. The Tory vote in 1945 was just on ten million. It too improved in subsequent elections, winning a record 13.75 million votes in 1959, the year of 'never had it so good'. In October 1974 the Conservative vote was just about down to its immediate post-war level, at 10.5 million. What once proclaimed itself to be the 'natural governing party' also seems to have failed to win fresh support, although seven million extra voters are available to be talked round to their way of thinking. This erosion of support for the parties from which governments have been formed since the war can be seen from the table below.

election	winner in terms of seats	share of votes cast %	votes won as % of all registered voters
1945	Labour	47.8	36.1
1950	Labour	46.0	39.8
1951	Conservative	47.9	39.6
1955	Conservative	49.6	38.1
1959	Conservative	49.4	38.8
1964	Labour	44.1	34.0
1966	Labour	47.9	36.3
1970	Conservative	46.4	33.3
1974 (February)	Labour	37.2	29.3
1974 (October)	Labour	39.2	28.6

There is one important technical complication about these figures, for those who are purists about statistics. The number of people who turn out to vote is usually affected by the age of the register of voters. People move, or die, or take holidays, and for such reasons the total electorate is often higher on paper than it is in practice. When the register is fairly fresh, as in the February 1974 election, a relatively high turnout (78.8 per cent that time) can be expected; as it becomes more out of date there is more room for error, and this goes some way towards explaining the 72.8 per cent poll in October of the same year. The remarks made in various places in this report about the low proportion of those eligible to vote who actually came out and supported a particular party or candidate can of course be qualified to some extent by discounting each calculation for the age of the register, type of constituency (people change address more often in some areas than in others), and so on. Even if this is done it will be found that the essential principles remain the same, and that the arithmetic is not altered by more than two or three percentage points. Far too many of our MPs — a majority of those who 'won' in both 1974 elections — do not have the proven support of anything like half of those eligible to vote, and a very great number are sitting in the House of Commons even though six or seven out of ten of their constituents are not willing to be represented by them.

Nor is this the only evidence that an increasing number of voters is dissatisfied with the politicians and major parties that are put on offer. The message is so plain that it overrides all arithmetical complications. For instance, the turn-out in the British general election of 1970 was 12 per cent below the turn-out in 1950 when an unusually high 84 per cent went to the polling booths. Taking the same twenty-year period, turn-out in most other industrial countries either remained steady or increased. (The information is published in *The Report of the Royal Commission on the Constitution*, 1973, Vol.II, page 34.) In West Germany, where one form of proportional representation is used, it rose very slightly, by 0.6 per cent to 86.6 per cent. In Sweden, where another kind of proportional representation is used. it rose by 9.2 per cent to 88.3 per cent.

Anyone who imagines that there is a long-term solution to all this in a simple return to the old-fashioned two-party system might profit from Fabian Tract No 211, published for twopence in May 1924. 'Our Electoral System suffers from temporary dislocation rather than permanent error', it said, '... as it is likely that within fifteen years the Liberal Party will be electorally defunct; we shall then be troubled with fewer of such multiple-candidate contests.' As can be seen more than half a century later the 'temporary dislocation' is at best a recurrent one and at worst something that is present nearly all the time. The Liberals may fade again, but it seems that they do return — and that Scottish, Irish and Welsh Nationalists are joining them. The two-party system has not really worked well for most of its ninety-year history — a fair appraisal would give it, say, thirty-five reasonably successful years out of the total. These would be between its inception and the turn of the century, and, stretching a point, between 1945 and 1964. After 1906 Labour was busy replacing the Liberals, or it was wartime, or there was a monolithic national government to meet a peacetime emergency; in none of these periods can it truly be said that two evenly matched parties were alone in the arena, each seeking to capture the favour of the electorate and each winning it in turn according to the swing of national opinion. It simply did not happen that way.

Never mind, say those who support our Bingo way of voting, it may be rough justice but at least it produces clear decisions. Britain needs strong governments, not woolly coalitions arranged after the voting is over. What such people must be asked is: what is so clear about a decision that produces a government that two-thirds or more of the people have not voted for? What is so strong about government policies that must by the nature of the system veer sharp left or sharp right after each election and then make a U-turn straight towards the centre again, as events take control, and our 'strong' governments are buffeted about like the unstable, inside-party coalitions they really are?

2   Playground battles

The 'winner-takes-all' or, as it is often called, 'first-past-the-post' system of electing candidates for Parliament is not only unfair, although that alone is a good enough reason for trying to improve it. The system is also divisive. It contributes to instability. What the governments it produces put into law is not necessarily what the people who are governed want. The significance of the individual MP is reduced. The power and strength of the political parties is unduly exaggerated.

The previous chapter set out to demonstrate the first of these propositions: that our present way of voting and counting votes produces results that are not fair. This chapter will discuss the next two: that the system is both divisive and a cause of instability.

There are three main causes of divisiveness in the way we vote. The first is that, in spite of the affluence acquired by most of the British people in the thirty years following the end of the second world war, class antagonisms persist. Too many peple are still poor. The questions often asked by those activists on the near left whose main motivation seems to be a wish to reduce or abolish inequality have not all been answered. The second cause is that although these divisions — some based on social status, some on income — may be wearing away (and possibly at an accelerating pace as prices shoot up, taxes remain high, and the spending-power of the better-off falls), the major political parties do not seem to be able to adjust to the change, at least while they are in opposition and during the first year or so after taking office. This is far from harmless; it is a period during which a great deal of damage can be and has been done. The third cause is that in their search for ways of managing the economy governments headed by both major parties have mistaken the will of the Trades Union Congress or the Confederation of British Industries, or abstract groupings such as 'labour' or 'business' for the will of the people. As a result they have brought these non-elected interest-groups right into the heart of Cabinet discussions; Parliament's function has been reduced to the act of giving formal assent to what is decided in this way.

Class conflict

The first of these causes — the existence of a disadvantaged class and the conflict that arises from it — has to be explained carefully because it can easily be misunderstood. It is difficult to produce an objective analysis of this particular phenomenon: nearly every reporter has an axe to grind. The starting point should be an acknowledgement of our relative wealth. There are many published figures (for instance in the annual *Social Trends*, published by the Government Statistical Service) that confirm what most of us know without needing to take the trouble of looking them up: that at least until the end of 1975, when we seemed to be heading downhill again, just about everyone in this country was more comfortably off than he or she would have been in similar circumstances thirty or so years ago. This applies to pensioners as well as home-owners, families on supplementary benefit as well as middle-class salary-earners. Whatever the measure the conclusion is the same. Even those who are unfortunate enough to find themselves out of work should be so provided for that for the first few months at least their net income is equivalent to or in many cases greater than their net take-home pay while working. This is shown in figures given by the Department of Health and Social Security in a Parliamentary Written Answer to a question from Mr Ralph Howell (Conservative, North Norfolk) on 16 July 1975; calculations based on these figures by Mr Samuel Brittan (*Financial Times*, 7 August 1975), amplify the point. This does not apply to those who while in work earn much more than £3,000 a year, or the longer-term unemployed, or those who feel that claims on the subsidy administration are undignified — but for most of those temporarily out of work it should do so, since a combination of tax rebates, family allowances, unemployment benefit, rent and rate rebates and other similar payments provides a social security safety-net that might have been dismissed as an impossible ideal by the wartime designers of our welfare state. In the 1942 report by the most celebrated of those designers, Sir William Beveridge, the level of hopes is set out clearly enough; the aim of social insurance, says paragraph 27 of that

famous report, should be 'guaranteeing the minimum income
needed for subsistence' — which is less than what is now
provided for. (Of course we provide at a generally lower
standard than European countries like West Germany,
Holland or Denmark, all of which have fairer voting systems
than ours.) The economic crisis precipitated by a combination
of the spendthrift policies of Mr Edward Heath's Conservative
government of 1970-74, the Arab decision to multiply the
price of oil by five at the end of 1973, and the spendthrift
policies of Mr Harold Wilson's Labour government during its
first eighteen months of office (March 1974 to August 1975)
may alter this picture over the next few years, but it is hard to
see Britain becoming as austere as it was thirty years ago.

Yet although the population as a whole has become
relatively affluent, the divisions between those at the top and
those lower down persist. The evidence of the Royal
Commission on the Distribution of Income and Wealth
(Chairman, Lord Diamond), published by the government in
July 1975, is that at least until 1973 the redistribution of
income was at most a slow and almost unnoticeable process,
while the possibly faster pace of the redistribution of wealth
was in no way revolutionary. This conclusion is modified if you
count social security benefits and other subsidies that help to
narrow the gap by improving the condition of the poor. Yet
there is no getting around the fact that some people are still
living in conditions worse than most of us would regard as
tolerable. The Glasgow slums and the worst areas of London,
Birmingham and Liverpool are a disgrace even in a Western
Europe that contains Naples. Other blights are well known.
Whatever may be said about the levelling effect of inflation on
the disposable income of the better-off, especially in 1974 and
1975, there is no doubt that some people continue to be in
need of assistance. As for the nearly-poor, those who might be
called 'not very well off', years of 'incomes policies' that have
purported to increase the income of the lower-paid have still
left many working-class families trapped in a life-cycle of a
kind that people in other groups within society would shudder
to contemplate.

For example, a table on page 139 of the 1974 edition of
Social Trends shows that the proportion of people who feel
that they suffer from a limiting, long-standing illness rises as

you go down the scale of social classes. About a tenth of the men aged between forty-five and sixty-four in the professional and managerial category report such illnesses; the figure for skilled manual workers is nearer to a fifth, while for unskilled manual workers it is nearly three out of ten. The government's *General Household Survey* states on page 279 of its 1973 edition that 'mortality statistics show an inverse relationship with social class', which means of course that the higher classes can expect to live longer. Many studies show that children in working-class families are less likely to do well at school than children in, say, middle-class families. The most comprehensive official study of reading ability, *A Language for Life*, published in February 1975, says on page 25 that 'the indications are that there may now be a growing proportion of poor readers among the children of unskilled and semi-skilled workers. Moreover, the national averages almost certainly mask falling reading standards in areas with severe social and educational problems.'

There are plenty of other such indicators for those who go about saying 'classes? I don't ever notice class differences' — all any such doubter needs to do is spend half an hour in a public library or, better, a quarter of an hour in the vestibule of a tower block of council flats. The people who live in such flats should need no convincing. Visitors to Britain rarely need to be told twice. But sometimes the British themselves are curiously unwilling to acknowledge the class differences that lie behind much of our political conflict. Perhaps the few examples above serve to make the point: when the 'left' or 'radicals' inside any party talk about the need for improvement, their prescriptions may sometimes seem unrealistic and their language may be unappetising, but there is something in what some of them say.

The social disadvantage that helps to fire a certain type of class conflict may be dwindling over the years, but there is still quite enough of it to constitute an ammunition dump for a great deal more conflict to come. As Britain moves through the new depression of the mid-1970s the class struggle, seen from the political activists' point of view, is apparently intensifying. There is a possibility that it could spread to a larger proportion of the electorate as each group fights for its share of a relatively smaller income.

Both major political parties are taking advantage of this.
Inside the Labour Party the call for more social spending and
more social control is often enough based on evidence of the
kind quoted above. Many Conservatives see the other end of
the same stick: they experience increases in rates and taxes,
which irk them. They are aware that universal welfare benefits
are sometimes paid to those who in all honesty could look after
themselves if they had to. There is strong feeling against a
financial structure that directs subsidies to well-off tenants as
well as those genuinely in need. There is widespread
muttering, by no means confined to Conservatives or the
middle class, against 'scroungers' who are thought of as living
on the state when they should be earning their own keep. Such
feelings cut across all parties and classes, as does compassion
for the badly-off, but it is not too much of an oversimplifica-
tion to say that the sense of outrage expressed by Labour Party
campaigners is most often at the condition of the poor
(sometimes extended to include the whole working class, which
means many who are not poor), while the sense of discontent
expressed by Tory activists is more often against the waste,
extravagance, and expense of indiscriminate benefits.

It is for reasons of this kind that the two largest parties so
often seem to go off the rails between elections. There are of
course other reasons: the Labour Party is heavily dependent
for funds and organisational support on the trade unions,
while large companies and business organisations will most
naturally (although not inevitably) assist the Tories. The
party/class conflict in its present form has its origins in the
events of 1930s, and a full exposition of the intricate nature of
what has developed into a series of mock gang-battles like
those so common in school playgrounds is properly the subject
of a separate report. But some of the consequences can be
outlined.

Party conflict
Before the Conservative government came to power in 1970 it
convened a policy meeting (one of several) at Selsdon Park.
One of the decisions associated with that exercise in
pre-election ideological planning was that taxes were too high
and that government spending should be cut. The social
services would have to be trimmed. New vigour would be

injected into commerce and industry by putting a stop to
coddling and protection. People, and business companies,
should 'stand on their own two feet'. There would be a return
to free enterprise and competition: the market, in the sense
understood by the witch-doctors we call economists, would be
given a chance to show what it could do.

After the Conservatives took office this planning was put
into practice. They carried out a fistful of social policies, like
increasing the price of school meals and abolishing free school
milk for children over seven, that seemed to the Conservative
faithful to be common sense but that were in fact ways of
cutting both the taxes paid by the better-off and the benefits
received at the lower end of the scale. (When the Labour party
won the February 1974 election it did not restore free milk to
over-sevens, and it soon put school meal prices up far more
sharply than had the 'Selsdon' Tories, but it simultaneously
looked after its own clientele-class by increasing payments such
as family allowances and introducing new ones like subsidies
on certain foods.)

Once in office Mr Heath, the new Conservative Prime
Minister, quickly discovered that however much his government might try to feed his apparently uncompromising new
doctrine to the nation, the nation would not keep it down. It is
important to understand why. Mr Heath's government was
certainly strong enough, in the conventional sense of the term
strong as used by those who aver that the Russian roulette
system at least produces strong government even if it is
sometimes a trifle unfair in its allocation of seats to parties. It
started with 330 MPs to the Labour opposition's 287, giving
Mr Heath's Cabinet an overall working majority in Parliament,
based on 13.1 million votes, not only one of the higher
Conservative turn-outs of the post-war years, but a
comparatively high 46.4 per cent of the votes cast. Mr Heath
won in spite of an almost universal belief that he would lose;
this gave him an initial extra charge of personal authority over
the government. He was convinced that he had been right all
along and that the policies in his party's 'abrasive' election
manifesto were what the nation wanted, or at any rate needed.
It is possible that he was misled by the electoral system, for in
spite of the apparent triumph that could be read into the
election results according to the existing rules, the hard fact is

that only one-third of the country's registered voters had marked their crosses against Conservative candidates — a post-war 'low' exceeded only by the two 1974 elections. Two-thirds of the country did not want a Conservative government, let alone the particular brand of Conservatism that had been worked out by an inner-party clique. What happened next should have surprised no one.

Half-way through his term of office Mr Heath was obliged by a combination of economic circumstance and widespread unpopularity to stand most of the new 'tough' ideology on its head. The Selsdon government became, as so many British administrations seem to in mid-term, a 'Butskellite' or middle-of-the-road government. The issue here is not whether particular policies or even the whole programme were right or wrong for the country at that particular time; it is simply that the ideas that Mr Heath and his chosen colleagues had thought up in opposition could not work unless a majority of the people wanted them to work. Mr Heath had believed that he and his fellow-Conservatives had been returned to office to change the course of the history of Britain, and in the single most lasting achievement of those years, Britain's formal accession to membership of the European Economic Community, he went some way towards meeting this claim — although Parliament's right to enforce this policy was challenged until the people endorsed it in a referendum. But the genuine Tory revolution that his Ministers spoke of turned out to be a futile hope. Britain in the 1970s would not accept radical change, or *apparently* radical change, coming from a single party associated in most people's minds with a particular class. A genuine popular mandate, which might have been arranged by gathering together everyone in all three national parties who believed in the mixed economy, might have stood a chance of winning-over a convincing majority of the electorate. Much of what the Selsdon Conservatives had wanted, although not all of it, might have been achieved in those circumstances; after all when you boil it down the programme was not so very different from the current practice of a government such as West Germany's, with its alliance of Social Democrats and Liberals.

In spite of the defeats of both the grand design of Selsdon and the party itself in two elections in 1974, the Tories have been slow to learn the lesson taught by events. Mr Heath's successor, Mrs Margaret Thatcher, started by taking most of her advice from a group of colleagues whose political beliefs seemed to be very like the Selsdon policy in its more fundamentalist form. Her own instincts appeared to be more sympathetic towards 'her' people — the striving middle classes — than towards other groups or the population as a whole. The people the left activists call the poor were all too likely to be labelled 'the feckless' by Mrs Thatcher. If enough of her people or other voters who wish to emulate them happen to be grouped in the right constituencies at the right time she could very well win an election and form a government on the basis of a large majority of seats. Can it be doubted that such a government would be no more 'strong' in the sense of being able to carry out its class-oriented policies than was the 1970 Conservative government?

The Labour Party has behaved in a similarly unprepossessing manner. Much of the social unrest of 1974 and 1975 can best be understood as the crescendo of a shock-wave beginning when those who voted with such hopeful enthusiasm for Mr Harold Wilson and his talk of the white heat of the technological revolution in 1964 and 1966 were so sadly disillusioned by the performance of his government under the pressure of adverse events in 1967 and 1968. A similar raising and dashing of hopes with the election and subsequent rejection of the Conservatives added to the general disenchantment.

While in opposition the Labour Party found its policy-making taken over by the activist proponents of class warfare. Their reasons were no doubt mixed, some wanting something very like revolution and some wanting merely to promote a greater degree of equality than presently exists. The Labour version of the Selsdon programme was a document entitled *Labour's Programme 1973*, which set out in almost every paragraph to emphasise the 'socialist' face of the party, in each case from a working-class point of view. The party's manifesto, published in some haste for the February 1974 election, was a much slimmer document that avoided saying very much, but some of the flavour of *Labour's Programme 1973* was retained with statements like 'it is indeed our intention to bring about a fundamental and irreversible shift in the balance of power and

wealth in favour of working people and their families'. Many
of the specific new laws and administrative decisions designed
to achieve this objective were drawn up with the active interest
and in some cases participation of representatives of the trade
unions, as part of the 'Social Contract'. The first signs of the
end of this red-blooded approach came in midsummer 1975
when the inevitable pressure on sterling forced Mr Wilson's
government to change course, just as Mr Heath had done
before him. A programme whose principal political purpose
was the maintenance intact of the Labour Party and the
cementing of its links with the trade union movement that had
founded it was, as so often before, jettisoned in order to meet
economic circumstances.

It will be seen from this necessarily rough sketch of the main
political trends of 1964-75 that at least in the first years of
office class pressures led our main political parties to start off
with policies that most people simply did not want. When they
did move towards more popular strategies, or programmes
designed to meet some urgent twist of economic fate, they did
so less out of conviction than in a panic obeisance to the advice
of non-representative authorities like the Civil Service or the
Trades Union Congress. Throughout that decade there was
never any sustained period during which the government was
consciously trying to carry out policies that had the willing and
proven support of a majority of the people. This, and the fact
that whichever party was in office their policies seemed to be
unsuccessful in solving our main economic and social
problems, is probably the main reason why the so-called
two-party system so visibly cracked in 1974.

Whether it ever worked satisfactorily is open to doubt, but
at least those who claim that it once provided clear-cut,
forceful government should be reminded that the Conservatives were in government, either separately or in coalition, for
all but nine of the forty-eight years between 1916 and 1964; for
a long while prior to that it was the Liberals who were most
often in charge. The Labour Party, on the other hand, never
really had control over the government until 1945; in 1924 and
1929-31 it was dependent on Liberal support, and during the
two world wars Labour Ministers were merely part of the
wartime coalitions. Mr Attlee's reforming post-1945 administration was mainly, although not entirely, imbued with that

spirit of understanding of what is and what is not within the rules (unwritten) of the constitution that is necessary if the old kind of democracy is to work. Much the same could be said of the subsequent Conservative governments; although the nationalisation of steel by the outgoing Labour government was thwarted, the Tories made no attempt to liquidate the new welfare state.

All this changed in 1964, with the advent of a Labour Prime Minister who placed the maintenance of party unity at the top of his order of priorities, above the need to bring his government's policies into line with what most Labour voters, let alone the electorate as a whole, might actually want; the fracture of the two-party balance was compounded with the arrival of a Conservative leader who was determined to abandon the 'Butskellite' policies of the past in favour of something more combative and distinctly Tory. Whether these new-style leaders were accidents of history, or whether they were responding to underlying changes in the nature of society could be debated at great length; the important point is that their arrival was more or less coincident with the visible breakdown of the old-world rules that had made two-party politics more or less tolerable.

The 'corporate state'

These two main causes of divisiveness — class conflict, and its perpetuation into at least the early years of government's terms of office — may set parts of the country against one another. The third cause, is paradoxically, the reverse of the other two, and it may help to explain why many voters are withdrawing their allegiance from politicians as a whole. To the politicians, one major lesson to be learned from the experiences of 1964-70 was that trade unions can break government policies. For this reason Mr Heath's government did its utmost to win trade union collaboration, as well as the cooperation of business interests, when it propagated its incomes policy following the freeze in increases in wages and prices in the second half of 1972. Mr Wilson, scarred by a clash with the unions during his previous term of office, did his own deal with the trade union bosses before the February 1974 election (precipitated by the actions of the National Union of Mineworkers), and all his decisions in government were marked by a determination to do nothing that would separate the trade union movement from the Labour government again.

The result is the development of a new form of government by an unrepresentative elite; its popular name in 1975 was the 'new corporate state', based on the apparent similarities to old-fashioned corporatist ideas in which representatives of various interest-groups, such as guilds, industries, trade unions, and the like, would together run the country. The irony is that it is just such a development that is thought likely to be made impossible by the system of voting we now have — while any change to any form of proportional representation has been castigated by opponents of such voting as most likely to lead to corporate representation and corporate-state government! This view of the possible consequences of proportional representation is argued forcefully by Ferdinand A. Hermens in *The Representative Republic*, published by the University of Notre Dame Press in 1958. Much of what is feared from a fairer system is in fact what we are getting now under Britain's unfair and unproportional system.

Many major decisions of government are taken in conclave by the leaders of the ruling party and the leaders of the trade unions, with business representatives having some say when the Conservatives are in office, and little or no say when it is Labour's turn at the wicket. This might have some substance as a political mechanism if the outside interest-groups were themselves elected in free and open contest, but the Confederation of British Industry is not even properly representative of British boardrooms, while the TUC simply represents the policies put forward by the most powerful leaders of its affiliated trade unions, without any direct or formal reference to the wishes of the rank and file. Some people believe that the TUC represents the interests of the people on the ground that it is truly representative of most British workers. The facts show how mistaken this is.

The total membership of the trade unions affiliated to the TUC is 10.4 million. This is just about a quarter of the number of registered voters. Women are a poor second within this fraction; the membership figures show 7.6 million men to only 2.8 million women.

None of the trade union bosses was elected to speak on specific political matters for the members, yet when they cast their card votes at annual meetings, or when they issue their powerful instructions to Cabinet Ministers, they do just that.

Most of the union bosses have been elected by tiny minorities on rules that seem almost designed to keep the ordinary day-to-day members out of it. For instance the trade union leader who was regarded throughout 1975 as the most politically powerful of them all, Mr Jack Jones, was elected general secretary of the Transport and General Workers' Union in 1968. Once in, he could stay until he retired at the age of 65. Some 334,125 members of the union voted for him, out of a possible vote three times as large. Thus only a third of the members of this giant union put in — once and for all — the man who, with the union's numerical strength behind him, was the architect of the Social Contract of 1974-5, the £6-a-week pay restraint policy that started in autumn 1975, and an unknown number of other government decisions taken on the basis that he seemed to be able to bring not only his own union but his colleagues among union leaders along with him. The President of the Amalgamated Union of Engineering Workers, Mr Hugh Scanlon, was elected by *six* per cent of his members in 1967. The General Secretary of the Association of Scientific, Technical and Managerial Staffs (ASTMS), Mr Clive Jenkins, is on a contract to his union's executive committee. The general secretary of the TUC, Mr Len Murray, is the collective appointee of union bosses of this kind, all strictly non-representative of the quarter of the British electorate that they are widely supposed to speak for.

There is evidence that people are catching on. A Gallup Poll published in the *Sunday Telegraph* in August 1975 showed that 61 per cent of respondents — a cross section of the public — thought that the views of the trade union leadership were not representative of the views of trade union members. When trade unionists alone were asked the question the feeling was just about as strong: 59 per cent said they thought the leaders' views were not representative of those of their members. And, asked if the unions were becoming too powerful, 52 per cent said in 1973 that, yes, they believed this was the case. In 1974 the figure had risen to 61 per cent, in August 1975 it was up to 73 per cent.

It is true that increasingly interventionist policies, pursued by successive British governments, have made sections of

Britain's working class more politically aware than they were in the years before 1964. It is not easy to avoid the sight of government Ministers kow-towing to trade union leaders or, more rarely, representatives of the CBI; anyone can see this kind of thing almost any night simply by switching on the television. The fact that this is where the power is flowing is widely understood; that it is not a universally welcome phenomenon can be deduced from the consistently recorded public opinion adverse to trade unions in their political role — while politicians are held in even lower esteem.

Before about 1960 the normal situation was that trade union members assumed that politics was best left to politicians, while trade union leaders were expected to fight for specifically industrial advances, like higher wages and better conditions of work. It was recognised that everyone had the vote, and that the right to form and use trade unions was unchallenged. The standard of living was improving; there was little drive towards battle with governments. One view of the way in which this has broken down is provided by Mr Anthony Giddens, who teaches sociology at Cambridge, in his book *The Class Structure of the Advanced Societies*. The way he sees it is that modern governments in many countries are trying to influence the actions of both trade unions and large-scale employers or 'megacorporations'.

Much of the impetus towards the development of capitalist planning, writes Mr Giddens, 'stems from the fact that, in certain respects, the state and the megacorporations have parallel interests in promoting stable and progressive economic development and in regulating inflation'. These objectives could be successfully pursued only with the involvement of the trade unions. The purchase price of trade union support, argues Mr Giddens, is likely to be a guarantee that the working class will reap its share of the benefits. As has been seen, the trade union movement has returned to its Victorian role as a political force.

All this removes power from Parliament and the power of choice from the people who elect members of Parliament. It does so in any country, of course, including, say, Holland, where there is long experience of nationally agreed incomes policies, and also a system of proportional representation. The difference in Britain is that there is no long tradition of successful political negotiation between the government and an interest-group as powerful as the TUC; the Dutch have been grappling with the intricacies of the matter for thirty years, and their diffuse society, with its religious cross-currents, differs in several important respects from ours. They have managed, by checks and balances, to avoid *control* by any one extra-Parliamentary group. Under the present electoral system we return either a Labour Party bound hand and foot to the idea of corporate-state negotiations, or a Conservative Party, many of whose members long to be able to do their own deal with the union bosses. In either case, experience shows that the governments thus elected are invariably turned towards this kind of extra-Parliamentary haggling with non-elected members of powerful groups.

Would a fairer electoral system make any difference? It could be argued that such a system would lead to a coalition of just those parties or sections of parties that most favour trying to reach agreement on incomes policies with the trade unions and employers. This is quite possibly true in Britain; indeed the wage control instituted by Mr Wilson's government after July 1975 was supported by a large portion of his party, and opposed by a rump of the left-wing *Tribune* group within it. The policy also received the support of the Liberal Party and the acquiescence of most of the Conservative Party, while Mr Heath, who started his term of office in 1970 in wholehearted opposition to such policies and later became a convert, was the motivating force for a group of Conservatives who wanted to support the government as strongly as they could. As a result Britain entered a period of quasi-coalition government in midsummer 1975, with opposition inside Parliament rendered less effective than ever.

Under a fair election system these different interests within the major parties would be out in the open; voters would be able to choose either between parties who favoured this corporate-state approach and those who did not, or between individual members of parties who leaned one way or the other. In effect Britain in 1975 found itself saddled with a kind of centre government, although not a satisfactory kind, anyway. Under a fair voting system the majority of the people would have decided whether or not this was wanted, and it might have influenced the form in which it developed.

It might be objected that, at the time the Labour government introduced its July 1975 incomes policy, the measures taken seemed to be very popular. This is true. The new policy was specifically designed to achieve consent, and the first indications from the opinion polls were that it had done so. One report, based on polling by Political and Economic Planning (*PEP Broadsheet No 553*, by W.W. Daniel, July 1975), was seen by various government departments in draft form while the administration was making up its mind about the shape its counter-inflationary policy would take. At the same time the fundamental objective of Labour Party unity was met by associating the Trades Union Congress fully with every part of the new policy: the very words used by the TUC in its own report were incorporated in the government's White Paper setting out its aim.

In this way the government did make an effort, at a time of economic crisis, to adjust its policies to what a majority of people might accept. This is to its credit. It does not vindicate the manner in which the government came to work out these policies, since at no time did a majority of voters have any direct say over what was happening. In the October 1974 general election the Labour Party was confirmed in power on a programme that was just about the reverse of what it started to do in July 1975. Voters were not consulted (except indirectly through opinion polls) about the change of direction when it came. There was no way of showing openly in Parliament the mixed feelings of the electorate, as might have been the case if fair voting had allowed the *Tribune* group on the left and the anti-wage-control Tories on the right a real chance to express their views, and by extension the views of those who elected them, in open opposition inside Parliament. The major parties swept all before them, for a brief moment united as any pair of playground gang leaders can be when they wish to prevent others from invading the turf.

Yet it is when the gangs revert to their normal games of rivalry that they cause the most disturbance.

Unstable government

The textbook claim that the single-member, 'mark your X and leave it to the party' system of voting now in operation provides 'stability' is no longer supported by the facts. The instability of

British society is the result of forces whose expression has been felt in other Western countries since the mid-1960s and it would be wrong to blame the electoral rules for creating the student and street-demonstration unrest that has become so familiar. The instability of British governments is another matter: this is, quite plainly, a consequence of the ping-pong nature of the two-party system in its present broken-down form.

For example, the National Incomes Commission set up by the Conservatives was abolished by the 1964 incoming Labour government — which then established a Prices and Incomes Board and Manpower and Productivity Service. This was abolished by the 1970 Conservative government which established the Pay Board and a great deal else besides, including the National Industrial Relations Court. These were of course liquidated by the Labour government when it returned to power in 1974; the Advisory Conciliation and Arbitration Service rose from the ashes.

The Industrial Reconstruction Corporation set up by the Labour government in 1967 was abolished by the Tories in 1970: no doubt the National Enterprise Board, appointed under a new Labour government law in 1975, will be rubbed out when the Tories next return to power.

Changes in taxation are equally dizzying. There is little chance for a company planning long-term investment to be certain that one form of regional incentive will last for a given number of years, or that the whole basis of taxation will be safe from comparatively sudden changes. The Labour government introduced Corporation Tax in 1965 in an effort to encourage companies to keep profits and use them for further investment; in 1971 the Conservatives changed to the 'imputation' system, moving back towards distributing profits to shareholders. The Labour government's 1967 Selective Employment Tax was discontinued by the Conservatives; the Tories under Mrs Thatcher have already vowed to abolish the new Labour government's capital transfer tax, which everyone pays on gifts over a certain amount. Pensions were switched between the late Mr Richard Crossman's scheme of 1968, Sir Keith Joseph's proposal favouring more participation by private pension funds, and a swing back to state pensions by Mrs Barbara Castle in 1974.

Some of the other 'you do it we'll undo it' changes are
familiar to most people. When in office prior to 1970 the
Labour government was in favour of Britain's membership of
the European Economic Community; in opposition the
Labour Party split in two and eventually, back in office again,
accepted the popular vote in favour. The back-and-forth on
incomes policy followed the same pattern. These changes,
coming as frequently as they do, are a symptom of the nervous
tension and instability that characterise Britain's major parties
as ordinary voters turn away from them.

This is not another way of saying that what is wanted is
government without change. The purpose of elections is to give
us an opportunity to change governments and therefore
policies. But the pace of change of policy experienced in
Britain over the past ten or fifteen years has been so rapid, and
so confusing, that it has contributed to industrial decline,
political instability and, by extension, social unrest. Some
people offer an intriguing case in favour of accepting all this
with equanimity: that it is a fortuitous means of smothering
the fires of revolution in the blanket provided by membership
of the Labour Party (or keeping reaction at bay by absorbing it
into the Conservative Party). If a fairer voting system led
initially to a government composed of parties leaning towards
the centre, this argument runs, the most extreme of the
radicals, reactionaries or revolutionaries might be drawn to
illegal or violent methods of trying to achieve their aims. The
activities of the extreme revolutionary bombers in Western
Germany might be adduced as an example. The trouble with
this argument is that it runs in circles: it says, in effect, accept
certain policies put across by means of an illogical electoral
system that is manipulated by determined people acting on
easily infiltrated parties, or they will get their way by some
other method. The correct approach, surely, is to change to a
system of voting that would leave the decision in the hands of
the people. All parties, of whatever view, would then have an
equal chance of winning them over; fringe-group extremists
would be seen to be in a minority. In any case, Britain has
recently experienced violence from groups such as the Angry
Brigade, not to mention the IRA, in spite of the existence of
two large, supposedly stabilising, political parties.

Meanwhile the quick-fire changes put across by successive

governments of both parties are doing a great deal of damage. They are a major cause of uncertainty: it is difficult for anyone to make long-term plans when there is no telling whether it will be possible to carry them out after the next general election — and elections seem to be coming around more often nowadays. This applies particularly to industry, whether it be nationalised or in the private sector. One Minister might object to the Steel Board's decision to close certain plants because the steel made there cannot be sold; another might accept the Board's case. One method of calculating taxation might put a company into apparent loss; another, introduced a few months later, will turn the same figures into a paper profit. At the same time there seems less reason than in calmer years to observe the law, at least in certain sensitive areas.

A trade union faced with Conservative legislation can wait for an incoming Labour government to repeal it; an individual faced with Labour taxes like the gifts tax can look forward to abolition under the Conservatives. Government policies and laws have become like plastic spoons and forks and soft-drink cans: something for use once only, then to be thrown away.

3 Charades

Another reason why Britain is becoming more difficult to govern is that Parliament so often fails to reflect the will of an increasingly volatile electorate. At least until they are forced by mid-term disasters to change towards policies that most people consider to be sensible, governments seem to be guided by the demands of the most vocal faction within the ruling party. Cabinets find themselves unable to exercise authority over powerful interest-groups, particularly if these are trade unions. There is very little room in all this for the people — that is, the voters as a whole, and not simply those abstract minorities (such as trade union members, factory workers, the middle classes, home-owners) who fill the minds of certain politicians when they equate their own supporters or clientele with the entire population of the United Kingdom.

Thus if good government is to be tested by whether it gives most of the people the kind of administration they want, at least for most of the time, the present electoral system is failing. There are, of course, other tests of good government. If the authorities please three-quarters of the people by oppressing the other quarter they can hardly be called beneficent. What happens to minorities is important, and this aspect of electoral reform will be discussed in later chapters. This chapter, however, looks at whether the policies the people of Britain get are the policies they would choose if they could. It also shows how the Members of Parliament that individual constituencies are saddled with are not necessarily the representatives that even their own party supporters would choose, if they had a choice.

The opinion polls constitute part of the evidence. They indicate that some government policies are opposed by overwhelming majorities of the voters, including majorities of voters who support the ruling party itself. Wait a minute, some will object. What is this about the opinion polls? Surely no argument that relies upon such evidence can be taken seriously by thinking people? After all, they do get all the election forecasts wrong, don't they? This is a widespread feeling, often expressed by people who in the next breath will quote the polls to support their own case on another matter. The feeling cannot be dismissed, however; for this reason there follows a short digression on just how seriously sample surveys of public opinion can be taken. The theory of survey techniques can be studied in one of many textbooks on the subject; a good one is *Survey Methods in Social Investigation* (Heinemann 1958), written by the present head of the Government Statistical Service, Sir Claus Moser, when he was a teacher at the University of London.

The polls in practice
The record of the opinion polls is far better than it looks at first sight. Most of them wrongly indicated a Labour Party victory in 1970, with the result that everyone except perhaps Mr Heath himself was amazed when the Conservatives won the general election of that year. They were mostly wrong again in February 1974, if forecasting which party is likely to 'win' is what they are to be judged by. And in October 1974 the polls seemed to suggest a far more convincing victory for the Labour Party than it in fact achieved. After the February 1974 election an 'apologia to *Daily Express* readers', by Louis Harris, appeared. 'In forecasting a five-point final lead for the Conservatives, with a consequent overall majority in Parliament, we of the Harris Poll could not have been more mistaken', it began. 'As the late Mayor of New York, Fiorello La Guardia once said, "if you are going to make a mistake, make it a beaut — but always admit it." So be it with us today.'

It is for this kind of reason that opinion polls are so quickly brushed aside when quoted in arguments. As predictors of how many seats a particular party will win in a general election their record has deteriorated since 1964 and 1966. Those dates give the reason. It is since then that the two-party mechanism has jammed up, and voters have turned away from the major parties and towards third, fourth and fifth parties. The relationship between votes cast and seats won has become more of a gamble than ever. It is now almost as difficult to predict the winner of a British election as to guess who will be the first to shout 'Bingo' in a crowded hall on a Friday night.

On the other hand, the record of the polls in estimating how the total vote will be divided between one party and another is as good as their record on seats won is poor. Taking the average of all the main polls published just before each general election since 1959, a number that has increased steadily over the years, the highest margin of error in predicting the popular vote was in 1970, when Labour's share was over-estimated by 4.4 per cent. It was in that election that many disillusioned Labour voters simply stayed at home, as most politicians now recognise. In every other election since 1959 the average error has been comfortably under 3 per cent and usually much less than that — although individual polls have sometimes performed less well than the average. The following table shows the polls' performance in detail:

election		popular vote %	polls' forecast* %	polls' error %
1959	Con	48.8	48.3	0.5
	Lab	44.6	45.3	0.7
1964	Con	42.9	44.6	1.7
	Lab	44.8	46.5	1.7
1966	Con	41.4	41.1	0.3
	Lab	48.7	50.4	1.7
1970	Con	46.2	44.0	2.2
	Lab	43.8	48.2	4.4
1974 (February)	Con	38.8	38.4	0.4
	Lab	38.0	36.2	1.8
	Lib	19.8	22.4	2.6
1974 (October)	Con	36.7	34.1	2.6
	Lab	40.2	42.5	2.3
	Lib	18.8	19.5	0.7

*Average of two polls in 1959, three in 1964 and 1966, five in 1970 and six in 1974. Derived from *The Polls and the 1970 Election* Glasgow: University of Strathclyde Survey Research Centre Occasional Paper No.7, 1970.

As further evidence of their value as measures of the general trend of opinion, the opinion polls showed consistently throughout the campaign leading to the referendum on

Britain's membership of the European Economic Community
that the public was divided more or less two-to-one in favour of
a 'Yes' vote. This was in fact what happened: the country as a
whole voted 'Yes' by 67.2 per cent to 32.8 per cent. It is true
that a great deal depends on the question asked: National
Opinion Polls showed in February 1975 that five different
forms of the referendum question would produce five different
results — from a 0.2 per cent 'No' majority for 'do you accept
the government's recommendation that the United Kingdom
should come out of the Common Market?' to an 18.2 per cent
'Yes' majority for 'do you accept the government's recommendation that the United Kingdom should stay in the Common
Market?' This February experiment also shows that the
opinion recorded by a poll can change fairly soon after it is
carried out. People do change their minds, and they are
influenced by what political leaders, especially governments,
say. Even so, the record outlined above suggests that when
opinion polls indicate that the people as a whole are
overwhelmingly in favour of this, or against that, by a very
large majority, it is wise to take them seriously, although
margins of a few percentage points on other issues might not
count for so very much. It seems fair to say that they can get
the broad outline of opinion at least roughly right, and that is
all that this digression has sought to demonstrate.

What the polls tell
On that basis, then, the polls can be used as one indicator of
public opinion on particular issues. In September 1974, for
example, *The Times* published the results of an Opinion
Research Centre poll showing that whereas in 1963 some 10
per cent of respondents thought that 'a lot more industries
should be nationalised', in 1974 the figure was 6 per cent.
David Butler and Donald Stokes show, in a table on page 280
of their *Political Change in Britain* (Macmillan 1974), that the
'yes' answer to the same question was 10 per cent or less in
1964, 1966 and 1970, although they report that many
individual voters changed their minds over the years. All the
many other polls on this subject have come up with the same
answer: most British people, including the overwhelming
majority of workers, do not want more nationalisation. Yet the
plans for the extension of public ownership, watered down

from *Labour's Programme 1973* because the party leader, Mr
Harold Wilson, understood well enough that this was the
public feeling, were not totally eradicated from his party's
platform, because that same Mr Harold Wilson understood
even better that the activists inside his party, as well as many
trade union officials, are as strongly in favour of more
nationalisation as the public (including most Labour voters) is
against it.

Not even the fact that the public felt at that time that 'trade
unions had too much power and influence over British
companies' (59 per cent of respondents) had any apparent
effect on the policies of the Labour government in its first
period of office. It is noteworthy that when National Opinion
Polls asked in February 1974, 'Who do you think is most to
blame for Britain's economic problems?' the answer from 42
per cent was 'the trade unions'. A year later it was 46 per cent,
a figure far outweighing the 18 per cent who blamed the
government and the 10 per cent who blamed employers.
Various subsequent polls indicate that the view has since
become even more widespread.

There is little need to rub in the point any more: all the
evidence shows that the proportion of the British people that
favoured the left-wing policies adhered to by the Labour
government between March 1974 and July 1975 is such a low
fraction that it could almost be called a fringe group. It is
certainly far less than the three-out-of-ten support for the
Labour Party in the October 1974 election; since on many of
these questions a majority of Labour voters is seen to be against
the left, overall support must be taken as well under two out of
ten — and on specific issues like nationalisation it is right down
to about six out of every hundred for, to ninety-four out of
every hundred against.

Once again this is not a purely party political argument.
The more extremely conservative of the Conservative
government's policies of 1970-74 were also unpopular when
measured by the polls, as were the abolition of free school milk
for children over seven, and the 'fair rent' scheme. National
Opinion Polls found much initial scepticism at Mr Anthony
Barber's 'give-away' tax-cutting Budget of 1972, and
subsequent economic events have indicated that the voters
were the better judges of the situation. On general attitudes,

the electorate has been more favourable towards the idea of companies disclosing a greater amount of information to their workers than the Conservative hierarchy has been. In September 1970 National Opinion Polls found four out of five voters in favour of such disclosure. This was still supported when it was thought to be a Labour far-left idea in mid-1975! The British public can often be closer to enlightened Western European practice than some of its political leaders. The Conservatives have been less than enthusiastic about a wealth tax: on 13 May 1974 an Opinion Research Centre poll published in *The Times* showed a 72 per cent 'yes' to the idea of such a tax 'to be paid by people who have more than £75,000', a figure much higher than the 58 per cent recorded in August 1969. Even 55 per cent of respondents recorded as voting Conservative were in favour. This does not mean that the Labour Party has no right to propose nationalisation, or that the Conservatives should not try to persuade the public that a wealth tax is a bad idea. It does mean that the voters should have a better opportunity to say clearly through the general election mechanism which kind of representatives — for or against nationalisation or wealth tax or whatever — they want to send to Parliament. At the moment they take the whole menu offered by the party of their 'choice', or nothing. There is no *à la carte*.

On the other hand it would be absurd to pretend that opinion is evenly balanced. On some issues the polls show, year in and year out, that the public as a whole is well to the right of governments of either party: two particular examples are hanging and immigration. Attitudes to trade unions are a mixture of disquiet and a desire to see more control over their activities; this does not usually extend to a willingness to sit out any disputes that may be the result of a single-party government's attempt to redress the balance of power in favour of industry and the taxpayers. On other issues, opinion is more volatile. Prior to 1972 intervention in industry or the imposition of some kind of incomes policy was associated with the left in the minds of many people; in 1975 the far left and the well-to-the-right opposed the growth of government involvement in the wage economy with equal fervour. Except on certain long-running issues like the treatment of prisoners, public opinion is not particularly stable over time. No voting system can make Parliament reflect accurately public opinion on every issue, or even, over time, public choices of priorities. Our nation is too complex for that; it is for this reason that the kind of person sent to Parliament must be as representative as possible of those who elect him or her. Governments have to govern, and it would be ridiculous to suggest that they did nothing that was not supported by a majority as recorded by the polls. Politicians have a duty to lead opinion, and there is much evidence from the polls to suggest that people will indeed follow the opinions of those they respect. Sadly, that respect is dwindling.

The best way out of this difficulty for militant democrats would be to find a way of making certain that at least at the beginning of every Parliament the membership was a reasonable mirror-image of opinion as a whole, and that the men and women making up this microcosm of British opinion were chosen by voters for their personal qualities and beliefs as well as their party labels. In this way there might be some hope of ensuring that a government's response to changing conditions throughout the life of a Parliament would not be too grotesquely out of line, for too much of the time, with what the majority of people wanted. What is needed is a situation in which it would be true that, in Burke's famous words, 'the virtue, the spirit, the essence of the House of Commons, consists in its being the express image of the nation.' As matters stand, this is a vivid description of precisely what we do not have. The next proposition constitutes another reason why this is so.

MP — or ventriloquist's dummy?
The British people are 'in revolt against the old ways of politics' wrote Louis Harris in the *Daily Express* of 26 February 1974. 'It is a people who sense a wider gulf between themselves and their leaders than ever before.' One of his polls showed that 'government, except for law enforcement, on the average cannot gain even one third of the faith of the governed.' During the election campaign Conservatives had complained by a margin of 60 to 24 per cent that they simply could not make their views felt on party leadership; in the Labour Party the margin was 56 to 26 per cent. The voice of the people was clearly heard in a survey conducted to determine public attitudes towards members of Parliament, reported Mr Harris. 'By 70 to 26 per cent, a sizeable majority want MPs who will vote against their party on a matter of principle, "even if that disagreement damages the party".' There were further large positive responses in favour of the notion that an MP

should have 'an open mind on problems' and that he or she should stick to their views even if they are unpopular.

None of this seems to be very easy under the winner-takes-all system in single-member constituencies. Voting in this way gives a very great deal of power to the local committee of the party whose supporters are most numerous in a particular constituency. Perhaps the most celebrated recent example of what this could mean is the case of Mr Reginald Prentice, Minister of Overseas Development, who on 24 July 1974 was told by the general management committee of his constituency Labour Party at Newham North East that he would not be wanted as their candidate at the next general election. Mr Prentice had not been convicted of any criminal offence. He had not voted against the Labour government on recent major issues. All he had done was make some rather aggressive remarks to the effect that he associated himself with the moderates within the party. On the same day, as news of the Newham North East Labour Party general management committee's decision was announced, the results of a special Gallup Poll were published in the *Daily Telegraph*. A random sample of 473 electors in the constituency, identified as Labour supporters, was questioned. In spite of widespread publicity in the newspapers and on television 28 per cent of these voters said that they had not heard of the anti-Prentice campaign inside their own party. Of the 72 per cent who had heard of it, 59 per cent were against the campaign and 57 per cent said that they preferred Mr Prentice as their MP to an alternative candidate more acceptable to the local Labour Party.

A case almost as celebrated in its day was that of Mr Nigel Nicolson, whose local Conservative Party at Bournemouth decided in 1958 to disown him following his opposition to the Conservative government's policy at the time of the invasion of Suez. He eventually persuaded his party executive council to conduct a postal referendum of all local members of the Conservative Association; this went against him by 3,762 votes to 3,671. The number of people who were able to participate in this choice compares interestingly with the twenty-nine to nineteen vote of Newham North East general management committee.

Not all such attempts are successful. Mr Nigel Fisher survived an attempt by the Conservative far right (the famous 'skinheads of Surbiton') to depose him in 1969 because of his liberal views on race relations, immigration, and Rhodesia. Mr Frank Tomney,

Labour moderate and Gaitskellite, survived half-a-dozen attempts by members of his own party to unseat him; the latest began after the October 1974 general election, in which he kept his Hammersmith North seat by a majority of 8,122. A year later he seemed more insecure than ever. But successful or not the argument always seems to be between different groups of party activists; the voters' choice is apparently the last thing that matters. When a strong-minded individual does go to the electorate for a verdict the results can be instructive.

For instance, Mr S.O. Davies, who became member for Merthyr Tydfil in 1934, was usually returned with majorities of something like 17,000 until 1969 when his local constituency party decided that at the age of eighty-three he should retire. At the subsequent 1970 general election he stood as an independent, winning 16,701 votes against 9,234 for the official Labour candidate, and with 15,479 as the combined vote of all three of his opponents, including Labour. It was a true overall majority. Mr Dick Taverne, Labour MP for Lincoln from 1962 to 1972, was returned by overall majorities in 1962, 1966 and 1970. In 1964 he won with 47.8 per cent of the vote. His constituency party officials came to regard him as too right-wing for their taste, and the break came when the party asked Mr Taverne to vote against British membership of the European Economic Community and he voted in favour. The officials decided against his adoption as Labour candidate in any forthcoming general election. Mr Taverne resigned, forced a by-election, and won with 21,967 votes in his favour as against 8,776 for the official Labour candidate, and 16,371 for all five of his opponents together. He won again in February 1974, although on a minority vote in a more or less even three-way split. In October 1974 Miss M.M. Jackson won the seat back for the Labour Party on a narrow 984 majority over Mr Taverne and (because of another three-way split?) only 37 per cent of the votes cast.

Two other similar cases are those of Mr Eddie Milne, MP for Blyth with 20,000 majorities from 1959 onwards, and Mr Eddie Griffiths, who represented Sheffield Brightside from 1968. Mr Milne was refused adoption by his constituency party in a vote taken in 1973, mainly because he had persistently demanded that the government should inquire into the corruption that he believed was affecting the Labour Party in the North East. He stood as an independent and won on a minority vote in February 1974, then lost by just seventy-eight votes in October of the same year. Mr Griffiths, who, like so many of the others, was considered to be not left-wing enough for his party activists, was defeated when he stood as an independent in October 1974, his left-wing opponent, Miss V.J. Maynard getting just about half the votes cast and, at 18,108 to 10,182 in a four-sided fight, a convincing majority over the rejected candidate.

These four examples are reported in greater detail in *When Rejects Re-run: A Study in Independency*, an article by A.D.R. Dickson in the *Political Quarterly* for July-August 1975. Mr Dickson writes that this kind of case is more likely to arise in the Labour Party than among Conservatives because in a constituency Labour Party decision-making 'is the prerogative of its delegate committees, whose members are representatives of ward parties or affiliated organisations, such as the trade unions.' When a local general management committee decides against an MP he can appeal to the National Executive of the Labour Party, as Mr Prentice chose to do, but there is no formal method open to him to consult the total membership of the party (although Mr Prentice took a vigorous come-back campaign direct to his constituency voters). In a local Conservative Association, the decision of the party's full membership can override any decision by a committee of delegates. Tory MPs who are dismissed or otherwise attacked by their local party can therefore appeal to at least the registered Conservatives (although this is quite different from giving the verdict to all the voters). As Mr Dickson remarks, rejected Labour MPs 'frequently feel that they have been unfairly dismissed by the vote of a small elite within the constituency party. Since they are denied the chance to appeal to all members of the party they take their case to the electorate.'

In certain circumstances this may work: the voters may be so loyal to a particular MP (as in the case of Mr S.O. Davies) that they will turn out for him in large numbers, particularly when they know he is unlikely to join the ranks of the opposition to his previous party in Parliament. In the long run, as the case of Mr Taverne illustrates, the desire to have, say, a Labour government can come to seem more important to many voters than the virtues of the man rejected by the party *apparatchiks*. The strong feeling that MPs should be independent spirits seems to lose out in the end to the slightly stronger feeling that after all when it comes to forming a government it is the party that counts. This is most likely when there is a small majority and people fear the effect of a split vote.

Another difficulty is that some party workers want their MP to be a straightforward delegate to Parliament, voicing his local party committee's thoughts in the House of Commons and never his own. Others stick to the more traditionally British view that an MP should be a representative, chosen for his general qualities and free to act independently when his conscience so dictates. The polls might suggest that the ordinary British voter is in two minds about this; the Gallup Poll in Newham North East showed Labour respondents replying by 50 per cent to 37 (13 per cent don't know) that MPs should vote according to their constituents' views rather than their own — while the same respondents were supporting him in his independent stand against his local party committee. Perhaps those who answered the Gallup Poll interviewers were quite clear in their own minds that there is a difference between constituents' views and the party's views.

These troubles are the product of the first-past-the-post system of voting in the single-member constituency. What militant democrats should demand is a system of voting that gives the individual the chance to choose just which type of MP will represent the party of his choice, without necessarily voting against his party as such. The various ways of arranging this by means of fairer voting are discussed in the next section.

PART TWO

Choosing better rules

4   The wide world
of fairer voting

Picking a better system of voting is not easy. For a start, there
seem to be so many of them. 'There are said to be some three
hundred systems of proportional representation in existence,
and the ingenuity of inventors shows no sign of exhaustion',
wrote the Treasurer of the Proportional Representation
Society, one J. Fischer Williams, in 1918. He was probably
right. If there were 300 schemes on paper then, there might be
400 or 500 or 600 now. Fortunately most of them are little
more than flourishes or variations on a very small number of
constant themes. More fortunately still, the choices open to
Britain today — impractical imaginings apart — boil down to
just five, and of these three can be fairly quickly run through
as possibilities to be set aside and brought out again only if the
better ones cannot be introduced because the vested interests
against them, such as the major political party headquarters,
are too powerful. This section sets out each of these five
practical possibilities for Britain in turn, leaving the best and
most intellectually attractive pair for last and working through
orders of desirability to those two.

This should not be taken as a roundabout way of saying that
when you come down to it only those last-discussed and
best-of-all systems (the double vote and the super-vote) will do.
The very first step on the ladder, the introduction of primary
elections, American-style, to decide which candidates the
parties should put forward, would be an improvement on the
present unfair and chaotic mess. If, after the argument dies
down, that is all we are left with it will still have been worth it.
Most of the other steps would be more of an improvement. It
would be a tragedy if doubts and hesitation and reformers'
internecine quarrels over which kind of reform there should be
left the British constitution unimproved and increasingly
vulnerable. That is what happened in 1918 when the
politicians nearly, but not quite, agreed on reform. We would
surely have been better off today if the reformers had not been
frustrated then.

Before going ahead with the steps up the ladder, two further preliminaries are necessary. The set of standards against which each possible new set of rules should be judged must be explained, and the existing rules must be briefly described. The standards are as follows:

1   *Is the system fair?* Does it provide a Parliament that reflects the wishes of the voters? It is important to be sensible about this. The most extreme example of proportional representation might lead to 635 members sitting in Parliament to represent 635 parties, a number that would be higher if there was room in the House of Commons for more. This is clearly ridiculous. The result would be fragmentation; the worst imaginings of the most ignorant opponents of fair voting would come true. The other extreme is the present British system, which usually (although not always) provides very unfair shares. This is also ridiculous. To avoid the first extreme, most, but not all systems of voting in other countries provide some kind of cut-off point. In Denmark, for example, it is necessary for a party to win at least 2 per cent of the valid votes cast (or fulfil certain other conditions amounting to the same thing) before it can be given one of the special seats shared out to make the Parliament as closely representative as possible. In West Germany the equivalent figure is 5 per cent. Under the 'single transferable vote' system the effective cut-off could be higher, depending on the form of the super-vote that is chosen. In Ireland, where it is arguably too restrictive, the number of unrepresented voters can be as high as 20 or 25 per cent. This is still much better than in Britain, where in most elections at least half the votes are wasted and third parties even with as many votes as five or six million hardly get a look-in in Parliament.

The rule-of-thumb for 'fair and representative' government in the assessments that follow will not be over-ambitious. Let us say that a system that provides for accurate representation in Parliament of the will of at least three-quarters of the voters will pass the test, while higher degrees of accuracy will be regarded as better — unless this is achieved at the cost of encouraging the formation of an unworkable multiplicity of small parties.

2 *Is the system practical?* Does it enable the voters to show
their choice of which party or parties they prefer? For this to
have significance in Britain the system must have some
significance in historical and cultural terms; something
completely foreign to our way of thinking would be less
practical than a method that can claim a link with traditional
roots in past electoral theory and known electoral practice.
This is one reason why political parties cannot be shrugged off;
another is that in a democracy containing forty million voters
you must have parties to organise and help to express broad
streams of opinion. The alternative would be an anarchic form
of democracy that would soon break down. The existing,
known parties might well be improved by change, but more
good might be done by a realignment between them than by a
political revolution that swept them all away at once.
'Practical' here also means making efficient government
probable. This is quite different from what is usually meant by
'strong government' when that term implies that a particular
Cabinet can more or less rely on its Parliamentary party
supporters to vote through, with varying degrees of obedience
and alacrity, almost anything it ordains. This is mythical
strength. If the country will not accept what is laid down by a
Cabinet elected by a minority of voters, or if extra-
Parliamentary pressures are always preventing the government
from working effectively, or if successive changes of
government mean successive unwanted reversals of policy,
then what we really have is quite the opposite of strong
government. A truly strong government is best produced by a
mechanism that makes it as responsive as possible to the
electorate, efficient, and able to take decisions that *last*
because political processes are held in greater esteem. Voting
rules that enable an electorate to choose which party or parties
shall form a government provide what is meant under this
heading by 'practical'.

3 *Does the system provide personal representation?* This term
is used by J.S. Mill in *On Liberty and Representative
Government* to describe the grand-daddy of the single
transferable vote, as put forward by Thomas Hare in 1859.
Mill, fired with enthusiasm, was delighted with the idea of
allowing the votes of the whole country to be counted at once,

with all of us in the same constituency, and Members of
Parliament able to draw support from whichever part of the
electorate would provide it. This might lead to the 635-party
Commons mentioned above under the heading 'representative
government' and can be dismissed as hare-brained.

In modern conditions personal representation can be taken
to mean that the individual voter has an influence over which
particular *candidate* is elected as well as which particular
party. This would also provide a choice between *factions* inside
parties. A voting mechanism that gave, say, the Labour voters
of say, Newham North-East a choice between Mr Prentice and
his leading left-wing challenger within the constituency, as
well as a choice between the Labour Party moderates and the
Labour Party *Tribune* group (which might be the same choice
all in one), would pass the first test of personal representation.

The second test of personal representation is said by many
MPs to be of special importance in Britain. This test is: does
the system preserve that special link between the member and
his constituents that is often referred to as a most valuable
feature of the British constitution? If not, does it provide a
reasonable substitute? The two tests cannot be separated. If an
MP is in Parliament in spite of the expressed wishes of most the
voters in his or her constituency then talk of a special mystical
link with the constituents begins to sound just a little hollow,
no matter how much good solid constituency work is done
between elections. The constituency work — taking up
complaints from individuals, answering letters, helping people
to meet officials, or to get proper service from government
departments — is, however, a duty that many people continue
to regard as essential. The best way to summarise the tests
under 'personal representation' is therefore: do most of the
voters feel that they have the man or woman they want to
represent them? Does the MP feel both willing and able to look
after everyone in a particular clearly-defined constituency?

4   *Is it technically sound?* There are two subsidiary questions
here. The first, important, one is, what happens when there is a
by-election? As we vote today there is no difficulty. The
constituency simply holds another election all on its own and
sends a fresh Member to Parliament under the same illogical
rules as before. Some of the proposed changes in the rules

would make this more difficult. The pattern of voting in by-elections when compared with general elections is, however, thought to be a useful indicator of what the people in general are thinking of the government of the day. So any new voting rules must also be judged by whether they maintain this assumed function.

The second technical question is, is the system easy for the voter to understand? Is the counting quick and easy? Would people be confused or put off by the unfamiliar? This test must be passed, of course, but its real significance lies only in its usefulness as a bogus argument against change. Any ballot papers likely to be adopted in Britain would be readily understandable by British voters, and while some of the counting methods are undeniably long and complicated, we do live in an age of computers. Provided that everyone who wants to can ascertain, understand, and accept the counting principles, the arithmetical mechanics of the matter need not be an insuperable obstacle to any system.

Winner takes all
These four standards of judgement — fairness, practicality, personal representation, and technical soundness — can now be applied to the existing rules for voting in British general elections, to see how well they work. Then we can go on to the possible improvements. The rules themselves need little elaboration.

The United Kingdom is divided into 635 constituencies. Since 1948, when the last of the two-member seats was abolished, each constituency has been entitled to elect one, and only one, representative to send to Parliament. The method of voting used is that everyone marks an X by the name of the candidate of his or her choice; the name of the party now also appears on the ballot paper. The candidate with the most votes wins, whether or not that is more than the votes of all the other candidates put together.

In practice, this means that in a majority of constituencies the election itself is a matter of form: these are the 'safe' seats in which it is nearly always certain that a candidate of a particular party will be returned because the area is by its social nature preponderantly Labour or Conservative. The effect is that more people are sent to Parliament by small

selection committees of political parties than by the voters
making a conscious choice of that individual. An election in
which a hundred seats change hands is unusual; if another
hundred are said to be in danger it means that in an average
general election about two-thirds of our MPs are in reality
chosen by the party caucus rather than by the voters.

This has the merit of linkage with our past: after all it was
the usual practice, between the sixteenth century and the
beginning of the nineteenth century, for seats to be held by
local interests of one kind or another. Two members were sent
from each constituency; they were more often than not chosen
by some kind of private deal. An election was not necessary
unless these bargaining sessions broke down. Many names are
given to the system of voting that we use to carry on this
tradition in modern guise: 'Winner takes all', 'simple
plurality', or 'first-past-the-post' are among those that are
better known. It should not take long to run it through the
four tests suggested above.

1   *Is 'first-past-the-post' fair?* The unfairness of the system was
described in detail in Chapter 1. It does not provide a
Parliament that reflects the wishes of the voters, although it
has a better chance of doing so when there are only two parties
than when other parties put up candidates for election. The
Liberal Party and the nationalist parties may attract fewer
votes at the next general election than they did in 1974 — who
can tell? — but even if they do that does not mean that the
two-party balance will have been restored and that the way we
now vote can be reprieved. For shifts away from the major
parties recur in waves (that was how Labour displaced the
Liberals after the first world war); these waves are likely to
increase in intensity as Britain's society moves away from the
old class divisions on which the present major parties are
based. Even now not all votes reflect true opinions because
some people fear they will waste their vote if they give it to a
probable loser. There is no way in which the will of at least
three-quarters of the electorate can be guaranteed representation in the House of Commons under the first-past-the-post
method of voting.

2   *Is it practical?* It is said that the single-member

constituency with simple plurality voting at least gives the
people of the country a straightforward choice of government.
This may have been superficially true in some elections
between 1935 and 1964 (although more people voted for the
losing side than the winning side in 1951) but with the decline
of overall support for the two big parties since then and the
collapse of the two-party mechanism in 1974, all that can be
said today is that the people get some kind of government —
whatever they choose. Some people equate single-party
government with practical voting, but it can hardly be said
that either the Conservative or the Labour Party is *in reality* a
single party; what is more, the truth of the parliamentary
situation after midsummer 1975 was 'that a Labour
government was willing to rely on Conservative support to get
its most vital measures through. The papering over the defects
of our present rules has become transparent.

A strong party system has great value. In *The Case Against
Proportional Representation*, the Fabian pamphlet published
in 1924, the author, Herman Finer, reminded his readers that
'The House of Commons talks and divides: the Cabinet thinks
and acts. Its touch with the country is as vital as its touch with
the House of Commons.' Various factors had already
combined to lead to the predominance of the Cabinet in
government, he went on, and the result, since 1867, was
'tightly to lace the Cabinet to the electorate by means of strong
party organisations'. Such a Cabinet, he argued, needs to rest
on a party organisation 'which is most vividly in contact with
the constituencies' — that is, where the individual member has
a clear and definite interest in his constituency. Then the
Cabinet, to be effectively responsible to the country must 'rest
upon the support of a *single* party'. This gave the voters a
straight choice between which of two governments shall be
returned to power. Then 'there need be no surreptitious
political bargaining between "ministrable" groups resulting in
contracts as to policy not submitted for popular ratification,
and which can be torn up by any of the contracting parties to
the detriment of steady and effective government, without the
country being able to hold them to their pledges'.

How odd this argument sounds half-a-century later, when
the system then so stoutly defended has just thrown up a quasi-
coalition Parliament, supporting a Cabinet out of touch at the

last election with at least seven out of ten of the voters — but instituting, within ten months of coming to office, a programme the reverse of what it offered at election time — and as a result of unspoken, if not quite surreptitious, political agreement with both the TUC and an opposition that was once supposed by most people to have turned against that very policy.

3 *Does it provide personal representation?* That the first-past-the-post system does not give the voter who is naturally anxious to see his or her party win any real choice between either individual candidates or factions within that party has already been shown in Chapter 2. Thus from the *average voter's point of view* the present way of voting fails the important half of this test. The second half, which is to do with the special link between the British MP and his or her constituents, is one that — on the face of it — the single-member constituency should pass fairly easily. Where there is a 'good constituency man' in the seat it does: such an MP will take a close and detailed interest in everything that happens in his constituency. He will be punctilious about attending his 'surgeries'. He will take trouble over letters from constituents, and he will be careful to give courteous replies to representations from interest-groups. He will stand up in Parliament to defend the interests of his constituents, even if it means little more than a few words about their difficulties in the midst of a debate at the end of which he will vote with the party line. Many British MPs strive towards this ideal, although it must be said that if the seat is especially 'safe' the need to nurse one's constituency may be less strongly felt than in an area where a small change of opinion will lead to a change of MP at the next election.

Now, several polls have shown that many people, possibly a majority, do not always know the name of their MP; even so, *from the member's point of view*, as well as from the point of view of those few constituents he meets as 'cases', a personal form of representation is quite possible in a first-past-the-post-type constituency. It may even be facilitated by the single-member device, although from the voter's point of view this is less true where allegiance is divided among three or four parties than among two. Of course the MP cannot represent the political views of those who did not vote for him. Still, a pass on the second half of this test; a fail on the first half.

4 *Is it technically sound?* The first-past-the-post method of voting is just as good, or bad, in by-elections as in general elections. In a straight two-party fight in a marginal seat it can show the trend of opinion for or against the government of the day; if more parties enter the contest the information sent by this method is nearly as clouded as it is when every constituency is voting. There is no more certainty at by-elections than at any other time that the MP sent to Westminster will represent a *majority* of the voters; this depends on how many candidates there are.

Is the system easy for the voter to understand? Everyone knows how to write an X. Enough people seem to be grasping the subtle consequences of this for a movement towards 'tactical voting' (changing to the party of your second choice if your favourite party seems unlikely to have any chance in a three-cornered fight) to have developed in recent years. There is also sufficient understanding of the futility of voting in safe seats for the turn-out to be especially low in such areas, and such a widespread understanding of the system's shortcomings that people have turned away from both major parties, and in many cases have given up voting altogether. A first-class pass on understanding.

5   The vote before the vote

A simple change that could be made to the present way of choosing Members of Parliament might — at first sight — seem to be the introduction of primaries. This would mean a special vote before the main voting, to decide who would be the candidates for the various parties. It would remove some of the power to select or dismiss candidates from party committees, and place it in the hands of party members or even, in some variations of the system, in the hands of all the voters of a particular constituency.

The idea behind primaries is that by and large the present single-member constituency, first-past-the-post way of voting works well enough, except for the glaring defect that in recent years party machines (especially on the left) seem to have fallen into the hands of small minorities. Most people are aware of the long-drawn-out battle for control in the Labour Party by pure socialists, as opposed to social democrats; some have discerned a parallel struggle between the Thatcher-Joseph and Heath wings of the Conservative Party. No democrat should object to an attempt by any individual or group to convert a political party to a particular way of thinking; what is objected to is that a mechanism exists whereby the conversion of a small number of party workers seems to be sufficient to override the wishes of the majority. What is wanted, instead, is a new set of safeguards, so that when it is alleged that 'this is what the majority wants' the proposition can be put to some sort of test.

There is a great deal of muddle about what this means. In the years 1970 to 1975 most of the public debate about small groups taking over local party offices, or other groups assuming a right to set party policy, was to do with moves initiated by left-wingers. So any change in the rules is thought, by both sides, to be a move designed to defeat the left. In 1974 or 1975 this would certainly have been true. But the reason why it was true is what really counts. A change in the rules might have hurt the left because the majority of the people, including the majority of Labour Party members, had not been convinced that the policies offered by the left were the right ones. The referendum on Britain's membership of the European Economic Community showed this plainly enough. The left wing of the Labour Party wanted a 'No' vote. It believed that this was what the people wanted. Powerful television performances by men such as Mr Anthony Wedgwood Benn and Mr Michael Foot helped its propaganda. It was also assisted by the active participation of several important trade unions, not to mention the official support of both the TUC and in theory that of the Labour Party headquarters, whose allegiance had been captured by the left at a special conference. It was aided, paradoxically enough, by a section of the Conservative party, a handful of Liberals, the Scottish Nationalists, Plaid Cymru, and politicians on both sides of the religious divide in Ulster. Yet the 'No' camp was defeated, overwhelmingly, in every part of the country and within every major party *including the Labour Party.*

Things could happen the other way round. A group within the Conservative Party could so shape policy that an attempt was made to cut down the Welfare State to a fraction of its present size — well beyond the trimming promised by Mrs Thatcher. This group could try to change the National Health Service into a mere safety-net for the very poor, returning most of the rest of health care to private insurance and the private sector. It could try to expand the private school system. It might wish to cut social security payments, or at least introduce more means-testing. Such a policy, with the many additional items that are easily imaginable, might seem very attractive to certain 'market economy' Conservatives, and it would presumably be compatible with some of the things that Mrs Thatcher has said about her own views. It is perfectly possible that a small group among the Tories could commit the party to such a policy, and that, by the luck of the draw in the first-past-the-post election system, a government committed to such a course could come to power on the votes of three or four out of ten of the electorate. If this happened it would be just as vital for true democrats to shout from the rooftops that this was not what the country had said it wanted as it was for them to say as much when the Labour dog was wagged by its socialist tail in 1974 and early 1975. The Liberal Party is not immune from a similar possible fate.

Primaries in America
In the United States, where primaries were invented, distaste
for manipulation by party workers or party bosses stretches
back to before the beginning of modern parties in the
republic. In 1763 John Adams described a caucus in Tom
Dawes' garret in a way that sounds very up to date in Britain in
the mid-1970s: 'There they smoke tobacco till you cannot see
from one end of the garret to the other', said Adams. 'There
they drink flip, I suppose, and there they choose a moderator
who puts the questions to the vote regularly; and selectmen,
assessors, collectors, wardens, firewards, and representatives
are regularly chosen before they are chosen by the town.'

During the nineteenth century the 'King Caucus' system,
which left nominations to the sitting members in each party,
was gradually replaced by a system of nominating conventions.
Party members would elect delegates, and the delegates would
vote on who should be the candidates. This did not work very
well: it was found that delegates could be bought and sold, and
that party bosses could manipulate conventions with little
difficulty; King Caucus still reigned. Towards the end of the
century conventions began to be replaced in Southern states by
direct primaries. In 1901 Wisconsin passed the first law
providing for primaries throughout a state; what became
known as the 'Progressive Movement' spread and within fifteen
years nearly every state had followed. There was little
uniformity. Each state chose its own form of primary. For a
British observer anxious to learn from the Americans, no firm
conclusions can be drawn from the experiences of any one
state.

There are two kinds of primary. In a *closed* primary only
members of a particular party can vote for candidates standing
(in America they call it running) behind that party's banner.
The law varies on just who is a party member. It is harder to
prove that you are, say, a registered Democrat in Mississippi
than it is in New York. In Alabama you had to swear in
advance to support whoever won the primary when the real
election came along.

The *open* primary, which is really a post-World-War-II
device, allows any voter to take part in the primary of
whichever party he likes, without having to say first whether or
not he is a member of that party. In Wisconsin you would be

given all the parties' ballot forms (with a list of names from Congressmen to dog-catcher) clipped together. You vote on the ballot paper of whichever party you like — and put the rest of the forms, unmarked, in a 'blank ballot' box. These blank ballots are never looked at but are destroyed at the start of the count. In most open primary states you can only vote in one party's primary at a time; the state of Washington allowed voters to participate in primaries of more than one party, while in California, for a while, it was legal for candidates to enter themselves in the primaries of both their own party and the opposition. Earl Warren became Governor after he won both the Republican and the Democratic primaries in 1946, and of course he thus won the election. In most states primaries are like mini-elections — they all take place, for all parties, on nomination day.

How primaries might work in Britain

Open primaries can probably be crossed off straight away, as it is hard to see British politicians taking to a system in which Conservative voters might influence the choice of a Labour candidate, or vice versa. In America this did lead to deliberate raiding: you voted in your opposition party's primary for its weakest candidate, so that he should be put up and lose.

Before closed primaries could be introduced another desirable reform would probably have to be accepted: fixed-term Parliaments. If a Prime Minister can call an election whenever he thinks he is likely to win, as he can now, there is little time available for the organisation of a primary campaign inside the three weeks' notice usually given for elections. One way round this might be to provide for longer notice — say six weeks — but no Prime Minister would like that, and most party officials would want to use the whole six weeks for a vigorous effort on behalf of pre-selected candidates. If it was laid down in advance that elections would be held on a prescribed date every fourth or fifth year, the primaries could be arranged well in advance, as they are in the United States. One objection might be the extra cost of having, in effect, two elections — but this could be controlled by proper rules for maximum expenditure, and it is not a serious obstacle for proponents of primaries to overcome.

David Watt, Political Editor of the *Financial Times*, wrote on 18 July 1975 that in his view primaries would be the best way to 'save and revivify the party system'. In a speech made after being pelted with flour at a rowdy meeting in Newham town hall in September 1975 the Home Secretary, Mr Roy Jenkins, aired the same idea; he was defending his Cabinet colleague, Mr Reginald Prentice, from a left-wing attack. The objection that MPs might feel inhibited by the possibility of having to face challengers for their seats at the end of every Parliament would have less force, Mr Watt wrote, if Parliaments ran for fixed terms of, say, five years. 'In any case, any feeling of restraint would be the consequence of genuine popular pressure and not of the blackmail of an unrepresentative clique combined with the manipulated loyalties of the rank and file.'

This would be true to the extent that British voters took to the idea. In many American primaries voting turn-out is so low that party officials can still make a great deal of headway by organising the votes of those who are for one reason or another beholden to them — as British party workers well connected with local authorities and local affairs might be in safe seats in either the city centres or the shires.

The average turn-out at American primaries is near to 30 per cent for run-of-the-mill primaries and 50 per cent in big set-piece primaries, like the one in Texas in 1970 when the conservative Democrats' favourite for Senator, Lloyd Bentsen, beat the liberal Democrat incumbent, Ralph Yarborough. Such major primaries usually decide the issue when party leaders split into opposing groups. If you took a turn-out of, say 40 per cent in a British constituency of 60,000 registered voters, that would mean 24,000 participants in the primary. Say 10,000 of them voted in the Conservative primary, 10,000 in the Labour primary and 4,000 in the Liberal primary. That would mean that 5,001 Labour voters, or as many Tory voters, or 2,001 Liberal voters could each choose who would be the candidate for their respective parties. In the case of the major parties this would be 8.5 per cent of the registered voters.

A strong clique with good powers of organisation could manage this, as the party bosses probably still do in many American local primaries. It usually depends on whether those bosses are united or not. Thus the Labour Party in Glasgow or the Conservative Party in Chelsea could still expect the 'endorsement' in primaries of the candidate chosen by the party executive, although this would not of course be so certain as it is now. And it would be possible to put up a good challenging fight in, say, Mr Prentice's constituency.

Where the law allows voters to 'write in' the name of a candidate not on the ballot form, as it often does, an organised group outside the party can beat the party machine. In the presidential primary of 1964, for instance, Republican voters in New Hampshire were given a choice between Goldwater and Rockefeller. The winner, on write-in votes, was Henry Cabot Lodge, at that time the Ambassador to Vietnam. He had not taken part in the campaign. Of course it did not win him the presidential nomination — Goldwater got that at the national convention, and a Republican débâcle was the result.

In especially safe seats the primary would be more convincing if a mechanism was incorporated to ensure that the chosen candidate had the support of at least half the party voters. In the southern states of America, where winning the Democratic nomination for many years more or less guaranteed a place in the Senate, the House of Representatives, or most local offices, they use the 'run-off' — if no candidate wins at least half the vote the first time round, the two with the most votes run against each other in a second primary. This would almost surely be necessary in Britain, where in safe seats there might be half a dozen candidates for the party's nomination, and in the first-round voting the leading candidate might have a third or less of the votes cast. If he were then declared the winner his base would not be much more credible to true democrats than if he had been selected by the party caucus in the first place. American experience shows that the run-off attracts large numbers of candidates willing to try their luck in the first poll. We could use the alternative vote (see next chapter) which would save the trouble and expense of a second round.

A third necessary ingredient of any British system of primaries would be a law regulating their conduct. This is not so simple as it sounds: British constitutional law has never really accepted the existence of political parties, and for many people the idea that legislation should control the way in which voluntary organisations conduct their affairs runs strongly

against the grain. Yet without any such law it can be taken
more or less for granted that the political parties would devise
rules for the conduct of primaries that would leave the real
power of choice of candidates pretty much where it is now: in
the hands of the parties.

In the United States the conduct of primaries is regulated by
law. Even so, in recent years, there has been a swing away from
primaries and back towards nominating conventions.
(Massachusetts is famous for its pre-primary convention at
which party activists say who shall run in the primaries!) It is,
after all, the grandest convention of them all that nominates
candidates for the Presidency, however influenced its affairs
may be by the results of the well-known presidential primaries
which take place in fewer than half the states. There could be
a similar disillusionment here.

These caveats are not intended as a dismissal of the idea of
primaries for Britain. The necessary reforms that would have
to accompany them — fixed term elections, run-offs or the
alternative vote for seats contested by more than two
candidates, and strict legal supervision would all in themselves
be welcome additions to our electoral process. In political
terms, it seems likely that the result would mean the putting
forward of some candidates more nearly reflecting the views of
the voters who support their parties than do many candidates
at present; there might also be room for the odd maverick, if
he was skilful enough. Mr Dick Taverne and Mr Enoch Powell
might still be in their respective parties. Beyond this, primaries
can be judged by the four tests outlined in Chapter 4 as
follows:

Are primaries fair?
For their limited purpose of giving party members a more
direct say over who shall be the candidates the answer is
'probably'. But primaries would not directly improve the
proportion between the expressed wishes of the voters and the
number of party representatives in Parliament. There might
be an indirect effect over a long period, since a system of
primaries that worked really effectively (and enticed many
more people to take an active party in party politics) might so
increase the acceptability of candidates that large numbers
would win overall majorities in their own constituencies.

Although this would mean fewer minority MPs it would not necessarily mean a fairer share of seats in Parliament. There would be no guarantee that at least three-quarters of the voters would have the parties of their choice represented in Parliament in fair proportions.

Are primaries practical?
Would they lead to better government? Primaries have the virtue of preserving what is valuable in political parties while restoring to the voters — or at least those who register as party members — some of the power of choice of who shall be the candidates of those parties. This might increase the efficiency of government, and its responsiveness to the electorate. But there is nothing in primaries that would ensure this; the idea depends more than most on the degree of enthusiasm with which it is put into practice.

Personal representation
Primaries could certainly affect who was the candidate of a particular party — but it must be said that this would not directly extend the choice to *all* the voters in a constituency, since only party members would vote. An MP dependent on primaries for his re-selection would have to think very carefully indeed about whether his actions in Parliament should be in the interests of his constituency as a whole, or just the party members within that constituency. As always, he would have to compromise; primaries might sometimes tip the balance in favour of the party rather than the whole electorate.

Technical soundness
There seems no reason why British voters should find it difficult to understand what primary elections are; the only difficulty might lie in arousing their interest. Before the experiment is tried, however, there is no way of telling what the response would be. As for by-elections, it would no doubt be reasonably easy to provide for a two-stage vote, with the primaries first and the full by-election following. The difficulty here might be that in safe seats the parties that knew in advance that they would lose might not want the bother and expense of two contests — but this might be overcome by the simple absence of candidates competing for the honour of losing.

In sum, primaries under certain controlled conditions might — depending on response — help to solve the problem posed by unrepresentative minorities taking over parties. This would be a gain, but the larger problem of unfair general election results, unrepresentative and therefore weak government, and the rest of the breakdown of our system would remain.

6 Second-chance voting

Three kinds of voting give you a chance to state your second, third, fourth, or later preference if for one reason or another you cannot have the candidate of your first choice. The best of these, and the only one that guarantees fair results, is the 'super-vote' (technically the 'single transferable vote') which is described in Chapters 9 and 10. Two less satisfactory forms of preferential voting are the 'second ballot', used in France, and the 'Alternative vote', which is used for elections to the Australian House of Representatives and most elections in the Australian states. (The super-vote is used for elections to the Australian senate, and the Tasmanian House of Assembly.) The two less-satisfactory systems are best taken in turn:

The second ballot
Say three candidates run for election in one constituency. None of them attracts more than half the votes. Then it seems reasonable to eliminate the runner with the fewest votes and let the leaders fight it out again. This is, in essence, the second ballot, recognisable as the run-off the Americans use when candidates crowd into their pre-election party primaries.

If more than three candidates take part the matter becomes that much more complicated. You could say that the second round is to be restricted to the two leaders whatever happens, as they did in Germany until 1913. You could say that anyone can enter the fray in either ballot, as they did in France before the second world war — or you could rule that only people who won more than, say, a tenth of the possible votes in the first round can have a second chance, as is laid down in the French constitution introduced by General de Gaulle in 1958.

The second ballot used by the French is essentially a product of their political instincts and methods, which are quite unlike ours. Their political parties are extremely volatile, many are short-lived, and there are large numbers of them. This is emphatically not a result of the use of proportional representation in France, since genuine PR has been tried only

in three French elections — all between October 1945 and
November 1946.

The French attitude to systems of voting is very imperfectly
understood in Britain. They are as fond of changing the rules
as we seem to be wedded to sticking to what we have. Between
1875 and 1958 France changed its electoral system *eight* times.
And, notes Dorothy Pickles, who reports this in *The Fifth
French Republic* (Methuen 1969), of the five different systems
used during that period only one was used for more than two
successive elections. Apart from 1945 and 1946 the French
have experimented with bastard systems in which first-past-
the-post voting has been mixed in with some proportional
representation rules.

For instance under the 1951 rules, which were to say the
least complicated, two different forms of proportional
representation were used for the Paris area and most overseas
territories (105 of 627 seats in the Assembly); the single ballot
system we have in Britain was used for a further twenty-three
overseas seats — no proportional representation there — and
for the rest of France and Algeria (499 seats, or the great
majority of them) they concocted an amazing system of
conscious disproportional representation under which if any
party or group of parties in an alliance won just one more
than half the votes, its list was given every single seat in a
particular multi-member constituency, which is the very
opposite of PR! This piece of clever mathematics served its
purpose of keeping the Communist and Gaullist representation
down to a minimum.

When not using such arithmetical devices, the French have
most often adopted the second ballot. It will be seen that the
way they approach the business of voting is very much their
own, and that, consequently, people who attack any mention
of proportional representation on the ground that it caused
political chaos in France are simply ignorant. Dorothy Pickles
reports a French estimate that between 1919 and 1957 the
average life of French governments was six and a half months
during assemblies elected by proportional or bastardised
proportional systems — and five months during assemblies
elected by majority systems, including the more or less
traditional second ballot system.

Because party allegiances (as distinct from allegiances to

specific trends of political thought) are so fragile in France, the often-used second ballot has served as a device for enabling squabbling factions to make up their minds who to support in the second round, once the first round has shown where the strength lies. This party horse-trading (*Kuhhandel*, or 'cow-trading' as the Germans called it when they used it under the Kaiser) has given the second vote a bad name; the rules of the Fifth Republic try to make the best of it.

Under these rules candidates in the 490 single-member constituencies are elected if they win half plus one of the votes cast, although these must add up to at least a quarter of the votes that could be cast if everyone on the register turned up. In 1973 only fifty-five of the seats in their Parliament were filled by such outright first-time winners. Everyone else had to go forward to a second round, although those who win fewer than a tenth of the possible votes in the first round are disqualified. In this second round all that a candidate needs to do to win is get the most votes, just as in Britain. The result in 1973 was that forty-five deputies were elected on less than half the total votes because even in the second round they could not get an overall majority. The second ballot does reduce the number of MPs elected on a minority of the votes, and it could eliminate them altogether if there were a stipulation that only front runners could go to the second round. The method gives French voters, many of whom are extremely sophisticated and knowledgeable about the finer points of politics, a chance to express themselves in the first round. It does not give proportional representation.

For example in the elections to the National Assembly of 4 March (first ballot) and 11 March 1973 (second ballot) only the Socialist Party, by coincidence, won seats in proportion to its 18.9 per cent first ballot vote. The three main government parties won only 23.9 per cent of the votes the first time, and some 31 per cent the second time — but 37.8 per cent of the seats, almost a British disproportion. The Communists won about a fifth of the votes both times, but only 14.9 per cent of the seats. The rest of the results were just as unfair. They have been worse in other years. The French constitution, which, with its separation of powers and its powerful stabilising presidential elections is completely different from ours (and from earlier French ones), may work as well with this as with most other devices the French have tried — but its relevance to British needs is very small.

Some British politicians have cast a shopper's eye at the second ballot. Would not defecting voters who protest by voting Liberal or Nationalist 'come to heel' on the second round? The large parties would like this. The answer is that there is no guarantee of what coming to heel would mean for any particular British party — the second ballot would not produce a Parliament that reflected British voters' opinions because (a) it is not proportional, and (b) in three-cornered fights everything might depend on how the Liberal vote was split, assuming the Liberals to be in third place. This might give some constituencies a Tory or a Socialist member when they would really rather return a Liberal. Swop the labels around as you please; the unsatisfactory result in British terms remains the same. In fact the second ballot is rarely suggested by would-be reformers in Britain.

Its brother, the alternative vote, has been taken very seriously indeed.

The alternative vote
The party horse-trading between ballots that is such a defect of the second ballot system can be avoided by asking the voter to say on his first and only ballot paper what he or she would do if there had to be a run-off. This means forgetting about the present X-marks-the-spot voting. Instead, the ballot paper is marked 1,2,3 according to your order of choice of the candidates. You might put a 1 next to the Tory name, a 2 next to the Liberal name, and a 3 next to the Labour name. If this is the way you vote you are saying 'If I can't have the Tory I'll have the Liberal'. Or you might mark the paper Labour 1, Liberal 2, Tory 3, or Liberal 1, Labour 2, Tory 3, or however you fancy. When the counting starts, all the papers are sorted according to first preferences. If no candidate has won more than the others put together the one who came third is eliminated. Then the second choices of the voters who chose that candidate are added to the votes of the other two. The winner will plainly have at least half the votes in his or her pile — just as in a second ballot that allowed only the two leaders to participate.

If there were only two candidates none of this would be

necessary. If there were more than two candidates you could have an interesting few minutes in the polling booth. Imagine the following extremely unlikely ballot paper, with instructions at the top to mark the order of your choice — 1,2,3, etcetera, up to as many as there are names:

Anthony Wedgwood Benn
(Labour, left)

Edward Heath
(Conservative, Mixed Economy)

Roy Jenkins
(Labour, Moderate Group)

Sir Keith Joseph
(Conservative, Free Market Group)

Jimmy Reid
(Communist)

Jeremy Thorpe
(Liberal)

John Tyndall
(National Front)

Many British voters might enjoy the chance to put a firm 1,2,3 ... down to 7 on such a list. Under the alternative vote it is at least *theoretically* possible. In British practice a list representing the various schools of thought within parties might appear in a small number of constituencies where the selection committee's choice was disputed, although when this system has been used elsewhere there have seldom been two candidates put up by any one party.

Nothing like this could happen in an ordinary, X-vote, winner-takes-all election. The Labour and Conservative Parties could not give voters such a choice between their different wings even in theory. For in present circumstances, faced with a three- or four-way split, most people simply vote for their own party, and some vote for the party they like second best if they think it has a beter chance than their own. If they vote for a maverick candidate they risk losing the seat for their party.

With the alternative vote it is possible to take the whole act of voting a great deal more seriously. The fanciful example above shows why. A socialist Labour party supporter would of course write '1' next to Mr Wedgwood Benn's name, the candidate under his banner — but where would the '2' go? To Mr Jenkins of the Labour Moderate Group or to Mr Reid the Communist? If one of those gets the 2 and the other the 3, will the 4 go to Mr Thorpe the Liberal or Mr Heath the Conservative Mixed Economy candidate? Equally a true blue Tory might not like the racial policies of the National Front, so with his or her 2 given to the other wing of the party this Conservative's 3 might go to the Liberal, and so on. The Liberal voter might be torn between the Labour and Conservative candidates — and so might give a 2 to the candidate who seems best in personal qualities.

The technical name for what is happening here is 'preferential voting' — and the act of voting is just the same as with the single transferable vote. (The differences are: (a) what they do when they count the votes, and (b) how many MPs are voted for in each constituency.)

With the alternative vote you stick to one member per constituency, just as now. When the votes are counted according to the alternative vote system the first thing is to see how many 1s, or first-preference votes, each candidate has next to his name. If someone has more than half the votes cast then that's it. He or she is elected. Everyone can go home. If nobody has a proper majority, the candidate who came last is eliminated. Since this is likely to be either the Communist or the National Front candidate in the above example, the votes thus taken off the bottom of the list will no doubt be very few. Anyway they are given to the other candidates, according to the 2s or second-preferences marked on their ballot papers. If this provides someone — probably one of the two leaders — with an overall majority (counting first preferences and the shared-out second preferences) then the counting can stop there. The winner is declared. If not, they will have another count, knocking off whoever is still at the bottom of the list and sharing out the vote according to the voters' second (or third) preferences among those who are left.

This is why the third preference might have some value. Say you voted for the candidate who came last, and your second preference turned out to be the one who came second-last. If the second-last one also has to be crossed off, then your vote might travel along to help the candidate of your third choice. It is as if you were asked 'Who do you want as your MP?' and then told — by the other voters — 'sorry, you cannot have him or her, but who do you want instead?' — and then, when you gave a second name, you were told, 'Sorry, not him either, but do have another go'. Your vote could keep working for you until someone had at least half the votes in your constituency, and then if you lost at least you would know that you had lost to half or more of those who voted in your constituency.

Preferential voting could have another advantage provided that the parties allowed it. If you are a Tory you could vote for the *kind* of Tory you like best (or if Labour the kind of Labour candidate you like best). There is no real danger of splitting your party's vote and letting the other side in, though the count depends on how many candidates there are altogether. If the other party's candidate wins in the first round of counting then that party would have taken the seat anyway, however the vote was cast — even in a straight X-vote election (although not necessarily in a super-vote election; see Chapter 9). If there has to be a second round and you happened to vote for the less popular of your party's candidates, then your second preference will probably make up for the lapse unless the count is over before they eliminate your first choice. No doubt your second preference will go to the other one of your party's candidates, if you feel that way, giving him or her full strength in the final count. In any case it would be surprising if the parties allowed their candidates to fight one another unless they had to. Yet the former Labour Minister, Dick Taverne, would have retained his Lincoln seat in October 1974 if there had been an alternative vote ballot. The official Labour Party candidate, Miss Margaret Jackson, won with 37.1 per cent of the votes. The 28.3 per cent who voted Tory would presumably have nearly all given their second preferences to the non-left Mr Taverne, who would have romped home, as most Lincoln voters would no doubt have preferred.

The most likely use of the alternative-vote method of counting preferences in England would be in three-cornered fights, with one candidate for each party, in which the supporters of whoever came third (and it could be Liberal, Labour or Conservative) would be asked, via the 2s on their voting papers, who they would have if their own preferred candidate could not win. In Scotland and Wales this could mean two rounds of counting in four-cornered fights, but it would only very rarely go much further than that.

The alternative vote in Britain

We very nearly had the alternative vote — twice. The method is always attractive to reformers who do not want to go as far as proportional representation. It gets round the absurdity of sending some MPs to Parliament on less than half the votes of their constituents. It is easily grafted on to the rules we already know; there need be no change in the existing constituencies.

The first time the alternative vote nearly came to Britain was in 1917, during the passage of what became the Representation of the People Act of 1918. The Parliamentary argument was fierce, following a recommendation by a Speaker's Conference (that is, a special committee of MPs set up by the Speaker of the House of Commons) that Britain adopt the single transferable vote in some boroughs and the alternative vote in others. In fact both systems were rejected, although it was a very close-run thing. (Four multi-member university seats used STV between 1918 and 1945.) At one stage in the Commons proportional representation was rejected, and the alternative vote put in its place by a majority of one — but after tactical jousting with the Lords everything fell through. The details are recounted in *The Electoral System in Britain 1918-1951* by D.E. Butler. Incidentally, the Labour Party wanted reform that time.

The second time the alternative vote had a sporting chance was in the Parliament of 1930-31, when Ramsay MacDonald needed Liberal Party support for his minority Labour government. A bill for the introduction of the alternative vote passed through the House of Commons. It was rejected by the House of Lords. The government could have sent it back again, but before it was able to it fell. There was another election, in which the National Government coalition won 554 seats to the opposition's 61. That was the end of any real prospect of reform at that time, although once again it had had the Labour Party's support.

Since 1931 the alternative vote has been suggested by various reformers on several occasions, the most recent being the attempt by Sir Brandon Rhys Williams, Conservative MP for Kensington, to introduce it in the House of Commons in July 1975. In a letter to *The Times*, on 19 June, Sir Brandon argued that 'if we introduced the alternative vote system, possibly on the way to a more elaborate voting reform in due course, it would have the immediate effect of turning members and candidates to the task of making themselves acceptable to the majority of their constituents'. This was preferable to simply turning out one's own party's vote. Many of its protagonists see the alternative vote as a first step towards more comprehensive reform: just get a House elected on this version of preferential voting, they say, and the better systems will follow.

The trouble is that this system does not guarantee any particular relationship between votes cast in the country as a whole and seats in Parliament. In *The Electoral System in Britain 1918-1951* D.E. Butler shows in a table on page 191 that on what seem to be reasonable assumptions about how the votes might have been divided up, the Liberals would have done better in elections using this system. But, he says, 'it would hardly have ensured fair representation all round, and it would not have prevented a party with less than 50 per cent of the votes from obtaining a potentially tyrannical parliamentary majority'. *The Economist*, in an extended analysis of the likely effects of electoral reform published on 2 August, offered the calculation that the Liberals would probably have won about fifty seats in October 1974, although their fair share would have been 118 or so. On the other hand the winning of the largest number of seats by the party that won the second largest number of votes in both 1951 and 1964 (February) would not have been prevented: these patently unfair results would probably have come out even more distorted. 'If fair representation is the object of reform, the alternative vote is no improvement', said *The Economist*. In other words, in terms of the parties' shares of seats in Parliament it could be at least as arbitrary as and possibly less fair than the simple first-past-the-post system.

A digression on single-member constituencies
It takes but a moment to explain why. The alternative vote is based on each constituency sending one member to Parliament

after all the first, second and possibly third choices have been worked out. If Labour piles up big majorities in its industrial strongholds it could win an impressive number of votes but — in proportion — fewer seats. The same could happen to the Conservatives with piled-up majorities elsewhere. Votes are not evenly spread throughout the country: some areas are more or less — it seems — forever 'Labour' and others appear to be eternally 'Conservative'. While these areas are divided into single-member constituencies, the composition of Parliament will be distorted, whether the votes are counted by Xs or numbered choices. Everyone who has thought about constituency boundaries can quickly see this. If the number of Labour voters in a town is about the same as the number of Conservative voters, and there are five MPs each representing one constituency in the town, everything depends on where the constituency boundary lines are drawn. You can draw the lines so that the Conservatives just outnumber Labour in, say, four out of the five constituencies, or you can draw them the other way, putting in just enough council estates along with the suburbs to have Labour win most of the town's seats. Our boundary commissioners are widely regarded as honest in this country, so these things are presumably a matter of chance. The unfair decisions may cancel one another out — but again this is a gamble.

So chancy is it, in fact, that the one thing that is certain is that *as long as each constituency sends only one MP to Parliament there can never be fair shares in Parliament.* When a constituency in the East End of London sends a Labour man to Westminster in every election, it means that working-class Conservatives, Liberals, National Fronters, and Communists in the East End are never directly represented in the House of Commons. When a Sussex constituency sends a Conservative to represent it every time there is a vote, it means that Labour supporters in Sussex, plus all the other parties' supporters, are never directly represented in the House of Commons. Excluding the London area, Labour has only seventeen out of 101 seats in the South East — 17 per cent of the seats, although 31 per cent of the voters in these constituencies support Labour. Likewise, in the West Midlands, the Tories, with 35 per cent of the vote, have only 19 per cent of the seats (6 out of 32).

It might be thought that areas of this kind cancel one another out so that the end result is fair shares. This very nearly happened, by chance, in 1892 — and even in that election it was only the two big parties, Conservative and Liberal, that were given more or less fair shares. The 1923 result was nearly proportional. The shares were out by just a hair's breadth again in 1951 — the only flaw was that the effect of the hair's breadth was that the Conservatives, with the second-highest number of votes, won the election in terms of seats. Thus it is, at best, a rare chance.

The alternative vote can magnify the distortions thrown up by any single-member-constituency way of choosing representatives. For instance, in a three-cornered fight in one constituency there could be a winner with just about one-third of the first-preference vote. Say the Liberals won the support of 35 per cent of the voters in a constituency, while the other two parties split the remaining 65 per cent, one getting 40 per cent and the other 25 per cent. The Liberals might capture most of the second preferences of the eliminated third party — and win.

If this kind of pattern was repeated, with variations, in a great number of seats, there would be a freak Liberal 'landslide'! If this is hard to follow, picture a constituency that has 60,000 voters, 40,000 of whom turn up and 13,000 of whom vote Liberal first time. That leaves 30,000 votes, which might be split, for the sake of argument, 17,000 Labour and 10,000 Conservative. Not many of those Conservatives are going to give their second vote to Labour, so it seems reasonable to say that the Conservative votes will be divided 8,000 Liberal to 2,000 Labour. The result would be: Liberal 21,000; Labour 19,000. Switch the Labour-Conservative labels round in this example and the argument stays the same. It would clearly be wrong and unfair to have a Liberal majority in Parliament on this basis — yet that is what the alternative vote could do. It is unlikely in practice, of course, but not impossible.

This built-in distortion is an automatic effect of the insistence on single-member constituencies. Some people think that this is an old British tradition; in fact the last multi-member constituencies were not abolished until 1948. The advantage of each constituency sending in three or four or

even five MPs is that it gives every group of any decent size in
any area a chance to vote for a representative of their choice.
This is discussed in greater detail in Chapters 9 and 10; for the
moment the important point to underline is that whether you
use X-voting or 1-2-3 voting there can be no proportional
representation with single-member constituencies as the only
voting method.

Is the alternative vote fair?
Thus the first of our four tests — whether the system is fair in
its allocation of Parliamentary seats — has plainly failed.
There can be no guarantee that the will of at least
three-quarters of the voters will be accurately reflected in the
House of Commons. On the other hand the alternative vote
might be used for some constituencies as part of a general
reform, as was suggested in 1918, and has been suggested
many times since. For example, if we had the super-vote the
whole country would be divided into multi-member constituencies. In places like London and Birmingham you could
draw a map of three, five or seven-member constituencies that
could be managed with little administrative difficulty. Yet
there would still be the problem of large, remote, sparsely
populated areas in, say, the north of Scotland, or the West
Country. If a few of these areas retained single-member
constituences with the alternative vote the overall effect on
representation need not fall below the standard of giving at
least three-quarters of the people of the country a fair measure
of representation by party. Voters in those single-member
constituencies would be less favourably treated than others,
but this would have to be set off against the possible difficulty
of creating geographically very large constituencies when
everyone in those areas might prefer smaller ones. They could
be asked in a local referendum.

Is the alternative vote practical?
It would be no more, and no less, practical than our existing
system. This is because it would be no less arbitrary. You could
get large majorities for single parties, but in theory at least
there could be some very peculiar results. On D.E. Butler's
assumptions, in the work quoted above, the Liberals would
have won more seats in most elections between 1923 and 1951,

but Labour's majority would have been even more exaggerated than it actually was in 1945, and the disproportionate Conservative/National Government majorities of 1931 and 1935 would hardly have been affected. The Conservatives rather than Labour might have won the 1950 election — although in fact Labour won the greater number of votes that time. These estimates are of course only as good as the assumptions on which they are based. There is no knowing how it would work in practice. Michael Steed gave a range of six assumptions in his calculations, published in *The British General Election of February 1974*, producing a table that gave anything from a Parliament with Conservatives the largest party with 277 seats to Labour's 275, to one with Labour ahead at 303 seats to the Conservatives' 220. It seems a fair guess that the alternative vote would produce single-party majorities almost as often as the first-past-the-post system, (*The Economist* estimates six times out of ten post-war elections) but since these would be not much less disproportionate in terms of overall popular votes won (and could be even more disproportionate) governments would be no more, or less, able to govern than they are now.

Does the alternative vote provide personal representation?
Some people would say that it does this better than any of the systems that are fair in Parliamentary terms. These will be people who are wedded to the idea of single-member constituencies until death do them part. It is certainly true that within each constituency the voters will have a greater say on who should be their MP than under the ordinary first-past-the-post method. No one can win who does not at the end of the day have more than half the votes. Candidates representing different factions within the same party could in theory compete against one another, giving voters the final say. Yet marks must be taken off for the lack of representation of the losing half of the electorate in each constituency. So if the alternative vote passes this particular test, it does so only according to the lights of reformers whose aspirations are especially modest.

Is it technically sound?
It is excellent for by-elections — better than first-past-the-

post. It is a good method of assessing what the first and second preference mood of the electorate might be at any particular time. There should be no trouble in understanding it; most British people can count up to ten, and they would rarely have to count past three or four. It could be used for by-elections as an adjunct to a super-vote system (Chapters 9 and 10), since that system, which depends on multi-member constituencies, cannot itself be used to replace a single MP who has died or resigned.

The alternative vote summed up

This reform could be introduced quickly, without the need to change constituency boundaries. It would remove the fear of the 'wasted vote' — you could vote your genuine first preference, secure in the knowledge that if that turned out to be attached to a loser your second preference would work for you. This would be a great advantage over the present system; voters' true opinions would be expressed. Yet the experience of Australia shows that the use of the alternative vote in single-member constituencies has not reduced the power of the major political parties over candidate selection. It has not produced fair shares for parties in the Australian House of Representatives — rather the opposite.

Many MPs in the Parliament elected in Britain in October 1974, sitting there on a minority vote, have discovered or will discover that they will risk losing their seats to the party that came second last time if the alternative vote is introduced here. We are certain, in such circumstances, to hear quoted once again the condemnation by Winston Churchill, made in the House of Commons on 2 June 1931, that the alternative vote was the worst of all possible schemes ... 'the stupidest, the least scientific and the most unreal'. The decision, after all, would be made 'by the most worthless votes given for the most worthless candidates'.

Thus for Britain the real usefulness of the AV might be as an appendage to a more rational reform, in areas where a better system might be awkward, such as in large rural communities — or for by-elections.

7 The straight party ticket

'Party list' systems of proportional representation like the ones used in, say, Holland, Italy and Israel are so alien to the British way of thinking that the busy British democrat should be fortified by good reasons before he bothers to look into them. There are two such reasons.

The first and lesser one is that there are many doubters who will say in discussions about voting systems something like: 'But we cannot have that here. Look at the inequities, complexities and muddles that result from the way they vote in Italy, or Israel'. They rarely mention Holland, Belgium, Denmark or Sweden, which have both good government and party lists, but they do often bring in France which may have workable government but certainly does not use a list system of proportional representation. It is useful to be able to reply, from knowledge, 'I agree. Nobody wants any of that here. What I am talking about is ...' and then go on to the mixed 'German system' (Chapter 8) or the super-vote (Chapters 9 and 10).

The second, more important, reason for acquiring some knowledge of the principles of these systems is that part of the mix in West Germany is a list mechanism, although it is thoroughly stirred up with British-style single-member constituencies. Since the German compromise is a hot favourite in Britain right now, the determined British reformer has little option but to work through the basic rules of party list voting.

People who really care whether or not parties choose candidates might also reflect that there is an element of humbug in the traditional British profession of abhorrence for the party list systems used on the European continent. Just who do we think chooses our MPs anyway? Before 1970 no party name appeared on our X-marks-the-spot ballot papers, and everyone had to remember the name of the candidate his or her party had put up. But it was the party that chose the candidate, just as they do with lists. Nowadays our voting papers are a little more honest, and carry party labels. It is still the party that makes the choice, and the hard fact is that the British voter has *no way round* this, while some party list systems do give a choice.

The theory of the list system is very simple. You vote with a mark next to the name of your party on the ballot paper. In this way you have voted for the whole list of its candidates. You might be in a five- or ten-member constituency, or one that is even larger; whichever it is your vote goes to your party. All the votes are added up, and then each party is given a share of seats corresponding to its share of the votes. The party with the most votes gets the most seats, the party with the second most votes the second largest number of seats, and so on.

There is method in this apparent Continental madness. The Belgians adopted the party list system in 1899, and it spread through much of Europe after that. It suited them because their division between Flemish and Walloon tribes was a constant source of friction. In this way each tribe's party could look after the interests of its own people. There was a clear system of fair shares of power between them. Holland, with its Catholic/ Protestant and Conservative/Socialist divisions found the scheme equally useful. The Dutch have always managed to keep their country together, and their tempers calm, because unlike the Northern Irish they have learned to share everything (trade union groups, businesses, political power, television stations) broadly three ways — between Catholic, Protestant and non-religious groups. The Scandinavians took up the idea, and made a great success of it. Weimar Germany also used it, with the unhappy result that the dreadful things that happened to that doomed republic get blamed on its electoral system, sometimes by people who know very well that the facts do not support this notion (see next chapter) but choose for the moment to ignore the social, economic and political factors leading to the rise of Hitler. The PR-elected governments have not solved Italy's problems — but the question arises, would any system overcome the Italians' present troubles?

For people not accustomed to lists the difficult part to understand comes when the votes are counted. It is all very well to say that each party shall get seats in proportion to its votes, but what happens if the ballot papers do not flutter down in a neat enough order? Say that the Conservatives, the Labour Party and the Liberals try for five seats in a Sussex multi-member constituency in a Britain operating the list system. If the votes added up to 50,000 and the Tories got

30,000, with Labour and the Liberals winning 10,000 each there would be no trouble at all: the Conservatives would get three seats for their list, Labour and the Liberals would get one seat each.

The sad truth is that life is rarely quite as neat as that. Take a four-cornered fight in which the Conservatives won 17,500 votes, with Labour attracting, say, 15,000, the Liberals 11,000 and a Nationalist 6,500. How do you divide the seats up then? The several answers could drive the non-specialist quite mad. They should not trouble British democrats, however, for all you actually *need* to grasp is why one of the two classic answers to this mathematical conundrum helps larger parties, while the other tends to favour smaller parties, and a third formula tries to bridge the gap.

The first is called the 'd'Hondt rule', Mr Victor d'Hondt being the Belgian who invented it. The essential principle is to make sure that when all the seats have been shared out the average number of votes needed to win each seat turns out to be more or less the same for each party. This is also called the 'method of the highest average'.

The second is called, dauntingly enough, the 'method of the greatest remainder', which is another arithmetical formula, designed to give each party seats according to how many votes they have won over and above the amount necessary to take one seat. This is the one that helps smaller parties; it would be adopted if we wanted to give Plaid Cymru or the fringe national parties a better chance. The other one — the d'Hondt rule — is for keeping the small fry out.

Thirdly, the Scandinavians have invented an even more complicated formula, designed to make sure that the big parties are not over-represented, while yet guarding against any encouragement to the very smallest parties to put up candidates.

It is not essential to follow the arithmetic, but for those who wish to do so the way the rules work is as follows:

The d'Hondt rule, or the method of the highest average
The vote-counters, or the computers, divide each party's vote by one, then by two, then by three and so on. The above invented example might turn out as shown overleaf.

	Conservative	Labour	Liberal	Nationalist
Total vote	17,500	15,000	11,000	6,500
divided by				
1	17,500	15,000	11,000	6,500
2	8,750	7,500	5,250	3,250

It can be seen from this table that the five winners can be read off after two divisions. You simply take the highest numbers of the table, in order, and give each a seat until five are filled, like this:

$$17,500 - \text{Conservative}$$
$$15,000 - \text{Labour}$$
$$11,000 - \text{Liberal}$$
$$8,750 - \text{Conservative}$$
$$7,500 - \text{Labour}$$

So the result is: Conservative, two seats; Labour, two seats; Liberals one seat; Nationalists no seats.

This result would be quite different if the count were made according to the next method to be explained.

The method of the greatest remainder
This time you start by working out a quota, which is done by dividing the total votes cast by the number of seats to be filled. There are 50,000 votes and five seats, therefore the quota must be 10,000. So each party gets one seat for every 10,000 votes it has won. You can write it down this way:

party	votes won	quota	seats	remainder of votes
Conservative	17,500	10,000	1	7,500
Labour	15,000	10,000	1	5,000
Liberal	11,000	10,000	1	1,000
Nationalist	6,500	10,000	0	6,500

So far, so simple. One seat each to the three major parties. But who gets the fourth seat? And the fifth? This again is easy: you simply read down the column of remainders. The Conservatives have the largest remainder here (7,500), so they get another seat.

The second largest remainder (6,500) is by the Nationalist's name. Thus they get the fifth seat — the one that under the d'Hondt rules would have gone to the Labour Party.

If this happened often enough in a seat like the one above the Labour Party might wake up to a wheeze the West Europeans thought of long ago: they could divide themselves into two parties, each of which might get 7,500 votes. This way they would have two high remainders, capture two seats, and squeeze the Nationalist out again. This fiddle cannot be managed under the d'Hondt rule. There are many such wrinkles to these party list vote-counting systems; the British democrat need not waste time on them unless he or she wishes to become a specialist.

The Scandinavian compromise

The division can also be done in yet a third way. This is the Swedish method. They do not divide by 1, 2, 3 as under the d'Hondt rule, but, believe it or not, by 1.4, 3, 5, 7, 9 and so on. The 1.4 makes sure that very small parties cannot get a seat — if you divide, say 50,000 votes by 1.4 the answer is 35,714 which is a great many votes for the first round. Dividing by the bigger numbers means that in constituencies returning very many members the large parties cannot hog all the seats. In our example above those with pocket calculators can work it out: this rule would give the disputed fifth seat to Labour.

Government under party list voting

All this information will no doubt serve to convince some readers that list-system counting is another one of those inscrutable Western European devices that plain British folk should not be asked to understand. Yet from *their* point of view it makes sense. One of the criticisms the ignorant often make of PR (as if one such pair of initials could cover such a wide variety of totally different methods of casting and counting votes) is that it leads to the election of many small parties and thus to unstable governments. As it happens, most of the Scandinavians have enjoyed such stable government over so many years that 'stolid' would be a better description!

For instance, Norway was governed by its Labour Party from 1935 to 1965 (excepting the time of Nazi occupation). In Denmark the Social Democrats have held office, alone or in coalition, for thirty-two out of the last forty-two years. The Swedish Social Democrats have run Sweden for the past forty-three years. The normally accommodating Dutch, whose political party groupings managed to keep their multi-party system astonishingly stable for half a century until 1967, have been buffeted by the modern questioning and quasi-revolutionary politics that have swept through the Western world since 1968. It has shaken them up, but the system seems to be surviving under a Socialist Prime Minister, Joop den Uyl, who not only emulates Mr Harold Wilson in his search for a consensus, but actually looks a bit like the British Prime Minister. The Belgians, whose innate tribal tension is supposed to have led many visiting politicians from the former Congo (now Zaire) to re-invent the joke that 'they are not ready for independence yet', have managed to keep together, and prosper.

The Italians, who have had one new government every ten months since 1948, can hardly be said to have enjoyed a successful post-war political experience, although since all those governments have been dominated by the Christian Democrats there has been some kind of continuity. Their special problem, is, of course, that the Communist Party has been in a position of growing strength for so long that it has been impossible for the democratic-minded left to form a viable opposition and thus an alternative government. The British system of voting might well have entrenched the Christian Democrats even more deeply; the French system of having a second ballot (which is in reality designed to give Frenchmen a chance to eliminate the Communists once they have chosen between the non-Communist parties) might conceivably have served non-Communist Italians better — but to people who have experienced it for many years the proposition that democracy = proportionality is hard to shake. Italy is in truth a special case; its failures are the result of specifically Italian social, economic and political circumstances, and this would be true whatever system of voting they chose to use. The same is of course true of Britain; it is just that here we can now see how a move to fairer voting might make it easier to tackle some of our many other problems, while removing some of the particular problems caused by sham two-fisted two-party scrapping. It would be foolish to suggest that the change itself would solve all our problems: this is the real lesson of the case of Italy.

Choosing individual members

In some countries using party list systems there is more chance for the individual voter to choose which *person* as opposed to which *party* should be the constituency representative than there is under the British system, in which of course there is at present no real choice at all.

In Belgium, for example, a typical voting paper looks like the racing page of the sports edition of an evening newspaper. There are all the lists, each one running down the long paper, with up to as many as thirty-three names on each. Next to each name is a little blank circle. At the top of each list is a bigger circle, alongside the name or list-number of the party whose list it is. You can simply fill in the little circle at the top of your party's list, and leave it at that. If you do, your vote will be counted as showing a preference for the party's candidates in the order the party has set them out, and when the party's seats are to be filled, they start from the top.

You could, however, fill in a little circle next to the name of a candidate you prefer, anywhere on the list. This vote will help to move your chosen representative a few places up the list when it comes to sharing out the seats. The top ones always get in, of course, because they have first call on the votes cast for the party as a whole. But it is possible for voters to affect the order lower down — always remembering that the whole list has been prepared by the party in the first place.

In most countries using this, or one of the other various devices for giving voters a greater personal choice of candidate (in some countries you *cannot* vote for the whole list but *must* mark your preference for one of the candidates on it), the effect is still that the parties get mostly the candidates they put on their lists, in more or less that order, elected to Parliament. But some voters are more individualistic than others; in Denmark, for example, just about half the voters show their personal choice of candidate rather than accept all the party line. It can be arranged under such list systems that the personal votes for candidates of a particular party are counted first — so that those with the highest personal votes are the first to be allowed a seat from their party's share. Only then are their 'excess' votes given to those on the list who were less popular, and these are sent to Parliament in the order the party originally ordained. It may not be perfect, but it does give

more choice than the British system. We can now apply the
four tests established in Chaper 4 to party lists as a whole.

Are party lists fair?
Surprisingly enough, they may not be. Few electoral systems
give absolutely perfect proportionality, and those that do often
tend to have disadvantages that outweigh the mathematical
tidiness of giving every party, however small, a proper share in
Parliament, exactly equivalent to its support in the country. In
Norway, for example, voters in the towns are slightly
under-represented when compared with country voters,
owing to the way constituency sizes have been arranged. At the
same time the way they share out seats (dividing at first by 1.4;
see above) makes it hard for parties with low support in certain
areas to win any seats at all in those areas. As a result the
governments formed after elections in 1965, 1969 and 1973 in
Norway were all based on coalitions of parties that together
had won the most seats, but not the most votes. The
disproportion was far less marked than it usually is in Britain,
but it did happen.

   To overcome this possible difficulty several countries have
introduced a device to make the proportion as exact as
possible. They create a special 'pool' of seats to be dished out
when all the counting is over, so that if the normal allocation
of seats has somehow not provided precise shares to each party
the differences can be made up. In Sweden there are
thirty-nine such pool seats; in Denmark there are forty. This
may be over-solicitous of the Swedes and Danes, for while
inequitable results like those in Norway can happen when the
mechanism is as imperfect as the one the Norwegians use, the
usual result in most list vote countries — whatever the type of
counting — is a fairly good reflection of the voters' opinions.
Adding a special pool of seats to make up possible
discrepancies may soothe tidy European minds; it is not always
essential.

   Of course all proper list systems pass the test of providing at
least three-quarters of the voters with their due share of
representatives in Parliament; they could not be called
proportional representation if they did not.

Are party lists practical?

They certainly enable the electorate to show which parties it prefers. Just which parties form the government may be a matter for bargaining after the vote is cast. This is for many people the heart of the matter. Many British constitutional theorists believe that a simple majority system, like the one we use, enables the people to choose a government. Of course it does not. Such theorists also believe that in countries that use proportional representation the result is usually a shared control of Parliament. This is often, but not always, true. Sometimes there has to be coalition, or a series of different coalitions, as a party with a minority of seats puts together support from different parts of the house for different items of legislation — party bargaining after the voting is over. This does happen in some party list countries. But in some of them, like Holland, the practice has now developed of parties saying before the election who they will be prepared to share power with if there has to be a coalition, and on what terms. This gives the voters greater direct choice of government as well as party.

Whether choice of government matters as much as some people think it does is another matter. In Britain, where parties speak and, in their first periods of office, act as if their purpose is to remould British society forever, it seems vital — although you have to bend logic until it breaks to imagine that British voters as a whole really choose their governments (it is the luck of the draw that does that). In countries where it is taken for granted that every administration must seek a pragmatic, widely acceptable, form of legislation the notion of different parties representing different social, religious, or economic groups bargaining their way forward in open Parliament is easier to accept. The choice of government remains important, but perhaps not in quite the British sense.

Do party lists provide personal representation?

In practice, very little. In theory, those that allow for a mark next to the name of the candidate the voter prefers — as against voting the straight party ticket — do provide some choice. The MP's relationship to his or her constituency varies from country to country; in some cases it is more likely to be a constituency that links together like-minded people (Liberals,

or Social Democrats, or Communists or whatever) than one
that groups voters by where they live. This increases political
representation but minimises direct personal representation.
Yet North European MPs *feel* that they represent their local
interests.

Are party lists technically sound?
When a by-election comes along, there need not be one. Under
many list systems all that happens is that the vacancy created
by the death or resignation of a member is filled by the next
name down on the list his party put forward at the previous
election. This would be unlikely to go down well in Britain.

Ballot papers would at first be confusing to British voters.
They can be long, and they can contain many names and
parties, and possible places to mark. We could learn, of
course, but it might take several elections before most of us got
it right. The counting is complicated, but less tiresome now that
we have calculating machines to serve us.

8   The double vote

The West Germans, who have since the end of the second world war developed a stable, prosperous and progressive democracy, have also chanced to develop a unique electoral system that, with modifications, might suit Britain very well. This is hardly surprising, because it is half-based on the British method of voting. It is, in fact, a remarkably 'British' compromise, of the kind that works. Single-member constituencies return their own MPs on the same first-past-the-post method as the one we use. Superimposed on this is the interesting half of the German mix: a party list system to make the end product proportional. Of the 496 members of the Bundestag — their lower house — exactly half are directly-elected constituency members, just like British MPs. The other half are party list members.

How the double vote works
If you were a West German voter in a general election your ballot paper would inform you, reading across the top line, that you have two votes. On the left-hand side of the paper would be a list of names and parties, against which you would mark your first vote. If you are a straight party supporter, as most voters in most West German elections are, you will simply make your mark by the name of your party. You need not feel any obligation to do so, however; as will be seen, it is quite safe to choose the *candidate* rather than the *party* of your fancy in this first vote, because your second vote is the one that decides how many seats in the Bundestag your party will end up with. So you might look down this first list and make your mark against the name of someone you would rather like as your constituency MP even though he or she might belong to a different party from your own. In British terms, this might give a Labour voter a chance to put his X against, say, Enoch Powell (as some Labour voters in certain circumstances may privately wish to do) as constituency MP without making any difference to whether in the end the Labour Party will have the

most seats in the House of Commons. Any reader who insists
on party balance in every paragraph might reflect that the
same fanciful example of Enoch Powell could just as well be
used for Conservative voters!

Having disposed of this first vote, the West German voter
will now consider the right-hand half of the ballot paper. This
shows a list of parties rather than people, although some of the
names put forward by each party will appear in smaller type
below the party names. (Incidentally, the party names will be
in the biggest type on both sides of the West German ballot
paper because they are not quite so finicky about that sort of
thing as we are.) With this second vote you put your mark
against your preferred political party without any quibbling.
That is all you have to do — in effect, instead of putting one X
as in Britain, you put two crosses and then leave it to the
computers to take over.

The first votes are counted just as in Britain. Whoever wins
the most votes on this count becomes the representative of that
constituency. It is quite possible to become a West German
constituency MP on a minority of the constituency's first vote,
just as it is here. In the hypothetical example above, any
British constituency in which Mr Powell stood could have him,
just as they can now, and on exactly the same rules.

The second votes are piled up right across West Germany
and each party is allocated seats in strict proportion to the
number of votes won. There are one or two complications, of
course. No party that has won less than 5 per cent of the total
votes cast in the Federal Republic is entitled to any of these
party list seats. This is a stricter rule than it may seem at first
sight. If it was applied in Britain in just that form with no
modification, then the Scottish Nationalists, with 2.9 per cent
of the total British vote in October 1974, would gain no list
seats. Neither would Plaid Cymru, with its 0.6 per cent, nor the
Northern Ireland regional parties, with their 2.7 per cent.

There are two ways of getting around this. The West
Germans do allow for cultural minorities; this could apply to
all our Celtic parties, although not to the Communists or the
National Front or other fringe parties that would not have a
hope of crossing the 5 per cent barrier in any British election
with opinion as it stands today.

The second way round the difficulty is for a party to win at least three constituency seats on the first vote. This too would let our Celts through. If we all voted the way we did in October 1974, it would give the Scottish Nationalists a further seven list seats. The Unionists in Northern Ireland might lose one seat, while the Welsh Nationalists might gain one. These changes would give them seats in Parliament in proportion to their total vote in the general election. It would be relatively easy for a small party to win three seats somewhere in the United Kingdom, for this would not require many more than 100,000 votes — assuming that constituencies are kept at their present size. But winning 5 per cent of the national vote would require 1½ million or more votes. Yet even winning three constituencies might be too much for our extremist fringe parties; after all they could do it now, if they could find the voters.

When the West German computers have discarded the very smallest parties in this way, they start dividing up the vote between the parties that have qualified. They use the d'Hondt rule; its mechanics are explained in Chapter 7. The important point is that it works against small parties. Yet the results certainly are proportional, and at least on the surface they have become 'fairer' with every election since the war, since the smaller parties have gradually faded away under the discouragement of the rules. In 1949 votes for parties other than the three that now represent 99 per cent of West Germany's voters amounted to nearly 28 per cent of the votes cast. In the 1972 election this figure was down to 1 per cent, having fallen in every election between.

Purists will argue, with some justification, that this apparent fairness is a myth, since under different rules more small parties might have had a chance of survival. The answer is that you always have to make a choice. A *wholly* proportional system, designed to be *absolutely* fair, might have those very disadvantages of weakness and division that opponents of reform wrongly ascribe to the *nearly* proportional systems that actually work very well and that by any measure come a great deal closer to any reasonable idea of fairness than the haphazard British system. What has actually happened in West Germany has been a steady absorption of the fringe parties into one of the mainstream parties — the Christian Democrats, the Social Democrats, and, very much the smallest of the three, the Free Democrats.

If the West German voters were really disgruntled about this, they might show it by keeping away from the polls. In fact the turn-out in West Germany has remained high: in 1949 it was 78.5 per cent, in 1953 it rose to 85.8 per cent, and in 1972 it was 91.1 per cent. The table shows how proportional — fair? — the results were in the 1972 federal election.

	seats in Bundestag			*share of*	*share of*
	constituency	*party list*	*total*	*seats*	*votes*
	%	*%*	*%*	*%*	*%*
Social Democrats	152	78	230	46.3	45.8
Christian Democrats	96	129	225	45.4	44.9
Free Democrats	—	41	41	8.3	8.4

Percentage poll: 91.1%

This table also illustrates another most important aspect of the West German system. Remember that half the representatives in the Bundestag are directly-elected constituency members, just as in Britain. When the computer allocates seats to parties according to the second vote, it does so for the *whole* Bundestag, not just the party-list half of it. Thus in the table above it would compute that the Social Democrats should have around 46 per cent of the seats because they won around 46 per cent of the votes. This means about 230 seats for that party, allowing for technical complications. But, the computer notes, Social Democrats have already won 152 seats off their own bat in straight constituency fights of the British type. This 152 is then subtracted from the 230 they should have. The result is 78 — just 78 party-list seats to be distributed among the Social Democrats.

On the same principle, the Christian Democrats were awarded 129 party-list seats to make up their fair share of 225 seats, while the Free Democrats, who did not win any seats in the constituencies, nevertheless attracted enough second votes to deserve 41 seats, which they got on the party list distribution.

What this calculation means is that the Social Democratic voters were concentrated in sufficient strength in certain constituencies to win 152 seats in the British way. (The Labour Party in the North or the Conservatives in the Home Counties, Liberals permitting, might be able to make a similar claim in an English election.) At the same time there were enough Social Democrats spread about in other West German constituencies to warrant a further 78 representatives for their party. (Conservatives in the North or Labour supporters in the Home Counties might wish that they too could be represented at Westminster.) The interpretation for the other two parties is similar.

There should be no disgrace in winning a seat through the party list rather than directly in a constituency, although in the early years some West German MPs did brag about their personal majorities as a means of reinforcing their arguments inside the Bundestag. And very popular candidates do stand out. In 1969, for example, Herr Schmidt won 61.1 per cent of the first vote in Hamburg-Bergedorf, even though the second-vote share for his party fell in that election to 56.5 per cent. Thus do West German voters make their preferences known. It has become a practice for the political parties of West Germany to give first priority on their party lists to candidates who also fight elections in the constituencies. In other words you might be the loser in a constituency vote in one Lancashire seat, but you would still find yourself sent to Parliament if you were high up on your party's list for Lancashire.

As a result German representatives expect to do much the same kind of constituency work as British MPs, and with their high salaries and office staff they are probably better qualified to do it. They are expected to be seen frequently in the constituency, especially if they are constituency members, but even if they are party-list members allocated to that region. They 'nurse' constituencies just as do British MPs, with surgeries on specified days, although just as in Britain some of them neglect this duty. They — or their secretaries — open large piles of post every day, much of it on personal problems, just as in Britain.

These local ties are encouraged by the computer programme. When it allocates seats between the parties, it also divides them up between Germany's ten states, or *Länder*. The 78 list seats allocated to the Social Democrats in 1972 were divided up by the computer, not the party headquarters, according to party strength in each of the states. Then each state party headquarters received its allocation of seats, handed out according to who was first on the list, who was second, and so on. The idea behind this is that the choice of representatives in the Bundestag should be kept as far as possible in the hands of the state party organisations rather than the great central federal party headquarters. In Britain it would mean that, say, the Scottish Labour Party would allocate Labour's list seats in Scotland rather than Transport House, Labour's London head office; the East Anglia Conservatives rather than Conservative Central Office would draw up the East Anglian list.

The computer also makes up for any under-representation between one region and another by dividing up the share of the national vote attributable to each party according to the votes won by that party in each region. As the weekly journal *The Economist* put it in its edition of 2 August 1975, West Germany's peculiar mixture ensures fully proportional representation between each party, between each region of the country, 'and for each region inside each party and each party inside each region'.

A small additional complication is: what happens when a party wins more seats on first votes than it is entitled to according to the computer's calculation of proportions based on second votes? The answer is — let them have the extra seats. In such circumstances the total size of the Bundestag is temporarily increased. In 1949 there were two of these *Überhangsmandaten* or extra seats. There were three in 1953 and 1957, and five in 1961. There have been none since, but it is of course technically possible that such a thing could happen again. It is an imperfection in the generally balanced mathematical structure of the system, but so far it has not made much practical difference. In Britain in October 1974 the Ulster Unionists won one more than their strictly proportional share of seats. Under this rule, they might have been allowed to keep it.

By-elections are taken care of in the same way as in most countries with party-list voting: there are none. The next man or woman down on the list steps in to take the place of the representative who has resigned or died.

How the double vote was invented

The history of election systems in Germany divides easily into three stages. Between 1871, when modern Germany was united, and 1918, members of the old Reichstag were elected in single-member constituencies. No one could win without an absolute majority; to ensure this the second ballot (see Chapter 6) was used, as it still is in France. During that half-century of more or less autocratic rule by the Kaiser, the Reichstag was hardly a proper, responsible Parliament; it was more a collection of factions, broken up according to region, religion, and ideology. In 1912, for example, there were twenty-one parties represented in the 397-member Reichstag. This was the result produced by a system very like our own, and certainly not one that could in any way be called proportional representation.

The Germans did try genuine proportional representation after 1919, and the rules of the Weimar Republic actually encouraged the establishment of small parties. Every 60,000 votes cast for a party qualified it for a seat; it did not matter if the votes had to be gathered together from all parts of the country to reach the magic figure of 60,000. Yet between 1919 and the final take-over by Hitler in 1933 there were never more than fifteen parties in the Reichstag, and the usual number was somewhere between ten and twelve. But the Weimar Germans failed, for reasons unconnected with their electoral system, to achieve a stable German democracy in what was after all the first real try for Germany in all its history. Hitler, it might be noted, never won an absolute majority of seats in the Reichstag before he assumed dictatorial powers; if anyone insists that the very special history of the Weimar Republic is of relevance to the discussion of systems of election in modern times it should be noted that under the British system Hitler would probably have been able to win a majority of seats in the tottering Parliament of the Republic.

The third phase of Germany's electoral history begins in 1948-9, when a Parliamentary Council drew up a Basic Law of the Federal Republic, under the watchful eyes of the occupying American, British and French armies. It was the

British who interfered most, because they could not get it out of their heads that the system of proportional representation used in the Weimar Republic had somehow been responsible for the emergence of Hitler and the Nazis. The strongest of the post-war German parties (leaving aside, in all this, the quite different situation in Russian-occupied Germany) was the Christian Democratic Party headed by Dr Konrad Adenauer. This party campaigned for a British-style system with single-member constituencies, and winner-take-all vote counting. It was argued that this was *personal*, as opposed to the completely impersonal Weimar voting. The party was quite right to campaign thus if all it cared for was its own short-term interest: it would probably have won the subsequent elections with handsome overall majorities. In the long term it might not have been so pleased: in the 1949 elections the Christian Democrats and the Christian Socialists, their allies in Bavaria, won 115 constituency seats topped up by only twenty-four party list seats, but in 1972 fewer than half the alliance's seats — 96 out of 225 — were won direct. They depended on the list for the other 129. None of this stopped the Christian Democrats from campaigning for British-style voting until at least 1969, when they first saw they would lose out unless they too could enjoy the benefit of proportional representation.

The Parliamentary Council, with the smaller parties pressing for proportional representation and the British military governors questioning just about everything, reached a temporary compromise, to be used for the 1949 election only. It was agreed that three-fifths of the seats would be British-style, while the other two-fifths would be filled from party lists, the whole to be in proportion to votes cast. Everyone was anxious to avoid the mistakes of Weimar. So the 5 per cent barrier against small parties was inserted from the beginning, although at that stage it was 5 per cent of the vote in any one *Land*, or just one constituency victory — a much lower barrier than it became later on.

This supposedly temporary compromise was developed in stages until it became the system in use today. Many changes made it harder than ever for small parties to get representatives into the Bundestag. It would be surprising if the West Germans left it at that. They are as accustomed to regarding their electoral law as something to be tinkered with, and if possible improved, as we are used to regarding ours as immutable, handed down from the mountains. One thing they have achieved beyond any doubt: they started in 1949 with eleven parties in the Bundestag (or ten if you count the Christian Democrats and their Bavarian allies the CSU as one) and four elections later, in 1961, they were down to three. This is how they have remained. In 1969 thirteen parties took part in the general election, but only the three major parties could clear the 5 per cent hurdle. It is indeed, quite possible that the third and smallest party, the Free Democratic Party, will be eliminated sooner or later. It just scraped over the 5 per cent hurdle (winning no constituency seats at all) in 1969, and although it recovered a little in the following year, it could easily be wiped out, leaving West Germany with a two-party system elected by proportional representation. Opponents of electoral reform can accuse the West German method of many things, but not of causing a multiplicity of small parties, or weak government.

Governments in West Germany
The first seventeen years of the Federal Republic were the Adenauer-Erhard years, the years of the famous economic miracle. The country picked itself up from the wreckage of the second world war. The Christian Democrats had no difficulty in governing, although they needed the help of minor parties, and usually the Free Democrats, to establish majorities in the Bundestag. This failed, in the sense of the by then normal governing coalition breaking up in 1966, when the Free Democrats decided to go into opposition. There they sat, all forty-nine of them, while the other 447 members of the Bundestag — the Christian Democrats and their previous opposition, the Social Democrats — joined together in a Grand Coalition that lasted until the following election in 1969. Since then the Social Democrats have been in charge, in alliance with the Free Democrats. Does this mean that the parties — and in fact the small Free Democratic Party — decided who should govern West Germany?

In 1966 it was of course the big parties that decided. They represented the overwhelming majority of West German voters. In 1969 the Christian Democrats lost votes but

remained the largest single political group in the Bundestag.
The other two outnumbered them. In 1972 it was made clear
during the election campaign that the Free Democrats would
ally themselves with the Social Democrats if necessary after the
votes were counted, and on that occasion there was less room
for doubt whether the goverment then formed was the
choice of the majority of the voters taken as a whole. The Free
Democrats increased their share of the poll from 5.8 per cent
to 8.4 per cent; the Social Democrats went up from 42.7 per
cent to 45.8 per cent giving the coalition an overall majority.
The Christian Democrats fell back to 44.9 per cent.

The last time that Britain produced such a clear-cut
decision, with the party that took control of the government
quite plainly the one chosen for that purpose by an overall
majority of the voters, was in 1935. How these matters are
judged must depend on what it is expected that elections
should do. Whatever the expectation, four points stand out in
any direct comparison between the practical operation of the
British and West German systems since the end of the second
world war.

1 In West Germany the number of parties has steadily
decreased, until there is now a simple three-party Bundestag
that could quite soon become a two-party one. In Britain the
number of parties has lately increased, with half-a-dozen
parties in Parliament and the old two-party structure in some
danger of breaking up.

2 In Britain the voters do not choose a government. This is the
product of very nearly pure chance.

3 The post-election bargaining between the German political
parties has been more closely related to the people's wishes
than pure chance: at least those doing the bargaining are
representatives whose broad modes of political approach are or
should be understood by those who vote for them.

4 Where political parties let it be known before the election
what their attitude to coalition will be afterwards, as in West
Germany in 1972 and in recent Irish and Dutch elections,
among others, the people have some real chance of influencing
the choice of government. (Of course, voters who support their
parties on everything except coalition cannot make this
distinction. But then there never is a mandate for every item

on any particular party's platform — in West Germany or
anywhere else. This is why the choice of party, faction, and
individual candidate is so important under any system.)

On the other hand when a small party like the Free
Democrats changes its political attitude without formal
advance notice and for its own internal reasons it can change
the government without much reference to the voters. This
might be said to have happened after the 1969 West German
election, although the astute voter could have discerned well
before election day that it would happen. Such manoeuvering is
a potential weakness of any electoral system (it happened in
Britain when Ramsay MacDonald split the Labour Party by
joining the coalition government in 1931) and the main
preventative is the likely wrath of any honest politician, not to
mention the voters. The Free Democrats paid the penalty for
this kind of politicking in 1966 just as did Labour in the 1930s;
both lost heavily in subsequent elections.

Weaknesses of the West German system

The first and overriding one is that it is almost as bad as the
British system when it comes to control by parties over who
shall stand for election. Like all list-based methods of voting,
the West German mechanism places the convenience of the
political parties — and the largest ones at that — above the
freedom of choice of individual representatives by the voters.

The West Germans have experimented with a form of
pre-election primary, American-style, but usually the number
of voters given a direct say over who shall be the candidates
high on the list is very small. All party members might meet at
a selection conference if there were not too many of them;
otherwise they elect delegates to such a conference, as in an
American convention. The process of candidate selection thus
becomes a matter that local party professionals can influence
or control. The use of the first vote can in theory overcome
this, but in practice the rules for the nomination of candidates
make it harder for the maverick. To stand as a constituency
candidate the independent-minded West German must collect
the signatures of two hundred voters. Only parties can
nominate candidates for the second vote, on the party lists,
and the rules for establishing a party to do this are strict. In

this respect at least the British approach is preferable: all you need here is the support of ten voters, plus £150 deposit.

The law on selection processes within parties is fairly meticulous in West Germany, requiring a secret ballot of a duly constituted party convention or committee to choose a list. It differentiates between established parties and new ones, making yet another hurdle for new or small parties to cross. The old parties know well enough how to ensure that the candidates are those of whom they approve. Their final list will be a politically sensitive balance between various interests — trade unions, regions, men/women (although women have so far done badly in federal elections), business and church organisations and the like. A tradition of weeding out below-standard or otherwise unsatisfactory members began to develop in the early years; this may have raised the quality of the Bundestag and given it a better image in the eyes of the electorate, but it all adds to the completeness of party control. It is important not to take this too far: nominees of the *Land* (state) party executives are sometimes defeated by party special conferences. But it is mostly these that have the final say over selection rather than the electorate at large. It is more formal, and yet more democratic, than the British system — but it cannot be called open, or favourable to the individualist voter.

A second possible fault is the size of constituencies. Since half the seats in the Bundestag are reserved for the list, West Germany's forty million voters must make do with 248 constituencies as against the 635 shared out among the United Kingdom's forty million voters. The average electorate in their constituencies is some 161,000 while the average in ours is 63,000. In many cases the members elected through the party lists share the work in the constituencies (the number of *voters* per member being 80,000), but those who see a great advantage in small closely-defined constituencies of the British type will consider this aspect of the German system to be a flaw.

Third, it is possible under the West German system for the parties to wangle a greater share of seats for themselves and their allies than they would if they played the game according to the spirit of their own law. This is done by using the first and second votes for different purposes, on an organised basis. Thus the Free Democrats could arrange with the Social

Democrats that all *constituency* seats in certain areas should be fought by their bigger ally, while *list* seats would be left open to the Free Democrats. Voters would be asked to vote Social Democrat on the constituency side of the ballot, using their first vote, and Free Democrat on the list side using the second vote. This 'tactical voting' was first advocated in 1969, by the Free Democrats, after the voters had tried it out themselves; it could be used by the present coalition in the Bundestag elections of 1976. What is really at stake here is the small but possibly vital share of votes that falls away when a minority party is in danger of being stopped at the 5 per cent barrier.

The double vote system judged

Our four standards, as established in Chapter 4, can be run through fairly briefly, given the above information.

1 *Is the system fair?* Yes, to large parties and, as it has turned out, to the great majority of the German people. It is tough on small parties, or splinter groups. But it certainly provides a Bundestag that reflects the party allegiances of far more than three-quarters of the electorate, with great accuracy.

2 *Is it practical?* West Germany's government is widely thought of as efficient, responsive to the wishes of most of its electorate, and well able to take decisions that last. This might be more due to the general belief in what they call the 'social market economy' — with the main parties differing on matters of degree rather than principle — than it is due to the electoral system, but at least that system has not worked to prevent the smooth development of what is by most standards an extremely prosperous and successful democracy. It may even have helped it along.

3 *Does it provide personal representation?* Not in the sense that the voter rather than the party can choose the representative. On this test there would be little improvement in practice — although some improvement in theory — on the British system. In the sense of the MP's notion that he has a special link with his constituency, British MPs will be hard to persuade that they do not have the edge here. But the facts suggest that West Germany's Bundestag members are not far behind.

4 *Is it technically sound?* To the voters it is easy to understand, or should be — although some British supporters of the single transferable vote wonder whether all German voters really appreciate what is meant by the second vote. The computers, if not all voters, can manage the d'Hondt rule all right; any mistake would be quickly spotted by the parties and rectified. (It has happened at least once.) The count can be completed overnight.

Would it work in Britain?

Any proposal to transfer the elements of the West German system to this country must start by acknowledging that their constitution is in many important respects different from ours. They have a federal structure, with a strict division of power between the Bonn government and the state governments. We may be on the way to that, but we have a long road to travel through Scottish and Welsh assemblies to British regional assemblies and on from there. They have essentially fixed-term parliaments; so far we have not. They have an abiding fear of splinter parties and extremist groups; we could be more relaxed about these matters and our hurdle need not be so high as 5 per cent of the national vote. Yet it would be wise to insist on some such protective device, or the British electorate, in its present fragmenting mood, might spawn more splinter parties than is wise if Parliament is to regain the respect of the nation. Fortunately, we have a great deal of other peoples' experience to draw on.

This experience could also be drawn on for other lessons. While waiting for regional assemblies in England we could at least insist, in any new electoral law, that local parties (carefully defined) would be responsible for the nomination of candidates on the lists in their areas. This would help to ensure that list MPs were tied to their localities. Again, it is possible to legislate for party primary elections, giving individual voters (or party members) at least some say over the choice of candidates. There could be further improvement if on the second-vote side of the ballot paper voters could mark which of several candidates on their party's list they preferred, although this might make the paper too complicated.

There are other pitfalls. As we have seen, the West Germans allocate their list seats only after subtracting the number of constituency seats won. This makes the Bundestag wholly proportional. But in the early years the Christian Democrats sought to keep the directly-elected constituency half of the Bundestag separate from the list-elected half. The list seats would have been purely additional. This would have meant that only half the West German Parliament — the list half — would be proportional. The Christian Democrats could hope to sweep the board in the ordinary first-past-the-post half. There would have been no subtraction of these seats before allocating the list seats. Fortunately the plan failed. There was a great deal of argument about this 'ditch' between the two halves of the Bundestag, however. It would be a pity if we in Britain had to go through it all again. With a 'ditch' our Parliament would be only half proportional, and thus less than half fair.

Many of these technicalities would no doubt be ironed out during any serious preparations for introducing a double vote system into Britain. Support for a version of this system has been developed inside the Conservative Party and elsewhere. The Conservative Action Group for Electoral Reform wants to keep the constituencies as they now are, but to allocate additional seats to those parties that are unfairly represented. It avoids the trap of the 'ditch' and (in one of its several versions of its proposals) suggests 400 constituency seats to 235 'additional' seats — very near to the 40 per cent given to the lists the first time West Germany tried for regional allocation of seats: it proposes area groups of ten constituencies each for this purpose. And, like West Germany the first time round, this Conservative group's proposal does not provide for any second vote. It simply takes the first vote as a vote for both individual *and* party, and makes the count twice, the first time to elect the constituency MPs and the second to allocate additional seats.

This kind of proposal has the merit that it seeks to change the outward appearances of the existing method of voting as little as possible.

Important refinements like the second vote could easily be added on, either in Parliamentary debate before the proposal became law, or later on. As Miss Enid Lakeman points out, in *How Democracies Vote*, J.W. Gordon suggested something of the kind to the Royal Commission on Systems of Election in

1910. On that occasion the idea was to fill every seat on a proportional basis, using the votes cast in the present single-member constituencies. This, however, would loosen the direct tie between MP and constituency that is said by some in Britain to be so valuable.

What would not be so easy (in any system other than J.W. Gordon's) would be the transition to a new pattern of constituency boundaries. If you had 400 constituency seats and 235 list seats that would mean redrawing all British constituency boundaries accordingly — and this takes time when you are fitting the size of constituency to an arithmetical abstraction based on the idea of one constituency per member. If you kept 635 constituencies and added enough seats for proportionality the House of Commons might be enlarged to 800 or 1,000 members, which would be too large. Any open-ended approach could have this effect; fixing the number of members would be far better but it would be necessary to divide the number of seats 60-40 or 50-50 to make the list large enough to overcome disproportions. This nettle would have to be grasped. You could not have a West German system without altering our constituency boundaries one way or another.

Again, with any British imitation of the West German system the Celtic parties would no doubt insist on rules protecting cultural minorities. They might suggest that the 5 per cent (or whatever the 'barrier') be calculated on a regional rather than a national basis, as they did at first in West Germany. It would obviously be far easier for the Scottish Nationalists to win a twentieth of the Scottish vote than a twentieth of the whole United Kingdom vote.

If we had had the West German 50-50 system in operation in October 1974, and allowed for the small Celtic parties, the House of Commons might have appeared as in the table on page 111.

The table assumes that the two largest parties will be slightly favoured, and gives them each three or four extra seats, plus a bonus of one to the Liberals. Among the losers in this hypothetical example might be the Northern Irish independent and the Social Democratic and Labour Party member — but they could make it on alliances of convenience with a larger party of their choice; alternatively the rules could be liberalised even more than this chapter has suggested.

party	vote %	seats won	made up of consti- tuency seats	list seats	actual result	difference plus or minus
Labour	39.2	254	160	94	319	−65
Conservative	35.8	232	138	94	277	−45
Liberal	18.3	117	7	110	13	+104
Scot. Nat.	2.9	18	6	12	11	+7
U.U.Unionist	1.4	10	10	—	10	—
Plaid Cymru	0.6	4	2	2	3	+1
Other	1.8	0	0	0	2	−2

9 The super-vote, in theory

In October 1974, a distinguished Conservative, Mr. William Clark, was returned for the constituency of Croydon South, with 57.9 per cent of the votes cast. There were 25,703 votes in his favour, 18,717 against, and 15,670 who did not turn up to vote. Leave aside those 15,670 non-voters and all thoughts about how many of them might have used their right to vote if (a) the seat had not seemed so safe and (b) the voting system was seen to be fairer. Look simply at the results as they came:

Clark, W.G.	(Conservative)	25,703
Nunneley, D.	(Liberal)	11,514
Keene, D.W.	(Labour)	7,203

Whatever your party, it is likely that if you voted in that election your vote would have been more or less useless.

If you support Labour you might have been one of the 7,203 voters whose X merely recorded that they preferred Mr Keene. Such an X is pretty feeble. It did not elect Mr Keene, or any Labour candidate. It might have helped to make a point about the total Labour support in the whole country, but it did nothing to secure a seat in Parliament for the Labour voters of Croydon.

Even if you are a Tory, the odds are that your vote in Croydon would have been unnecessary. Why? Because Mr Clark could have defeated the runner-up — the Liberal — with just 11,515 votes. So 14,188 Conservatives, of which you could have been one, had no practical influence on the election to Parliament of the Conservative MP for Croydon South.

These extra 14,188 votes did have some psychological value. They showed that Mr Clark had a majority over his two opponents combined (although not all of them were necessary for that). They were also a measure of the undoubted strength of Conservative opinion in Croydon South. But that is all: the practical value of your vote, if you were one of those surplus Conservative voters, was nil. Mr Clark did not need it. No other Conservative benefited from it.

Adding up the wasted vote in Croydon South you get: Conservative, 14,188; Liberal, 11,514; Labour 7,203 — total 32,905. That is three-quarters of the votes cast!

Maxi-constituencies

This also happens in Labour- and Liberal-held seats. It is repeated everywhere, in every British election, with an average of more than half the votes wasted every time. As the British government told the Northern Irish electorate in an official leaflet produced in advance of the 1973 election in Ulster, 'In a single-member constituency all the votes not cast for the winning candidate are wasted, since they have not been able to elect anyone. And so are all the votes in excess of a bare majority cast for the winner, in the sense that they have had no effect on the result.' This is the inevitable consequence of having only one MP per constituency.

You do not get round it with the alternative vote (Chapter 6) because, although that system guarantees the winner an overall majority, it still does not produce any representative for the supporters of the losing candidate.

The West Germans keep single-member constituencies, but join their losing votes together in their party list. This is fine for political parties, but what about the voter? The super-vote could be the answer. But it depends on having multi-member constituencies.

For if a group of neighbouring constituencies is joined up to produce, say, a five-member maxi-constituency, there is a good chance of giving most of the voters, if not all, a useful vote. This is because the supporters of parties that would be losers in each of five single-member constituencies can be gathered together to return at least one or two representatives of their choice.

In Croydon, for example, you could join the neighbouring constituency of Beckenham to the existing four Croydon constituencies (Central, North East, North West and South). This would make a reasonably-shaped South London constituency, not all that much larger in area than the existing neighbouring constituency of Orpington, and smaller than the neighbouring constituency of Sevenoaks. Of course its voting population would be much larger — but then it would be returning five MPs.

In October 1974 these constituencies, taken together, had 99,864 Conservative voters, 68,912 Labour voters, and 43,717 Liberals. Two 'fringe' candidates won 1,500 voters between them. The non-Conservatives outnumbered the Tories in this supposedly 'true-blue' part of the country by 14,265 votes cast. Yet the five constituencies returned five Conservative MPs. The very least that any fair-minded person might expect would surely be a return of two or three Tories, one or two Labour MPs, and one Liberal.

Again, in areas like Durham the unrepresentative monopoly is in Labour hands. In the past people have comforted themselves with the notion that unfair results in various parts of the country cancel themselves out in general elections. The first chapter of this book shows that they do not. The super-vote is one way of making certain that results would be reasonably fair for multi-member constituencies in every part of Britain.

The single transferable vote

The technical name for the super-vote is the 'single transferable vote', because you get just one *single* vote — but a vote that can be *transferred* from a candidate on whom it would be wasted to one for whom it will do some good.

Why a *single* vote? After all there are to be three, five or seven MPs for each constituency; why not give each person three, five, or seven votes? Anyone who remembers the old-style local council elections will know the answer. If there are three candidates to be elected and everyone has three votes, then those three votes will usually be given in a block to whichever party you favour. That means that whichever party is ahead in votes takes all the seats. The unfairness is multiplied by three.

In our hypothetical five-member maxi-constituency of Beckenham and Croydon, the 99,864 Conservative voters would naturally give their five votes to the five Conservative candidates, while the Labour and Liberal voters would of course vote their own party tickets. The results would probably be: Tory 99,864 times 5; Labour 68,912 times 5; Liberal 43,717 times 5; others 1,500 times 5. The Conservatives would sweep the board — and the 114,129 non-Conservative voters would be just as unrepresented as they are now.

Why a *transferable* vote? The answer follows from the reasoning so far. If you were one of the Conservative voters whose vote was not needed to elect the most popular Tory in your five-member constituency, then your super-vote would move over to help the candidate of your second choice. It might be the second most popular Tory, or it might be a Liberal. But your vote would move — just as, when you are filling one of those ice trays for the refrigerator, the water overflows when it has filled one little ice-cube and moves to fill the next. It would be a useful vote.

If you were a voter whose candidate was clearly a hopeless loser — then, again your super-vote would be transferred to the candidate you like second-best, so that it becomes useful. If your second-choice candidate did not need your vote, or could not win even if he or she had it, your vote would move on again, according to your third choice — just as the water cascades down the ice-tray as each cube is filled.

In the counting-room, your super-vote ballot paper may literally whizz back and forth. It is a fascinating process. The important point to remember is that although your vote may not stand still, at the end of the day it can *only support one candidate.* So even if those 99,864 Conservatives all voted solidly Tory they could not by themselves take all five Beckenham-Croydon seats. They would probably get three, but might only get two. This is because the method of counting is designed to make certain that everyone has a fair share of seats, based on a certain quota of votes, explained below. But first consider how you vote in such an election.

Casting the super-vote
This is 'as easy as 1,2,3' said the British government leaflets handed out in Northern Ireland in 1973. A drawing of the face of 'PR Pete', a smiling child, next to these words showed that they must be true! The pamphlet advised: 'You should really study the lists of candidates (in the newspapers or the election literature) well beforehand and make up your mind about your preferences among the candidates and parties. There will probably be quite a number of names on the ballot paper. They will be shown in alphabetical order, and the parties they belong to will be shown. When you get your ballot paper,

mark the number '1' against the name of the candidate you most wish to see elected... Then ask yourself, if you cannot have your favourite, or if he doesn't need your vote, which other candidate you would like to see elected; put a 2 against his name. Then a 3 for your third choice and so on.'

This is very like the alternative vote (Chapter 6). In fact the Australians call both the alternative vote, which they use for elections to their House of Representatives, and the single transferable vote, which they use for elections to their Senate, 'Preferential voting'. There are two vital differences. The first is that with the alternative vote you have only one MP in each constituency — with the result, in Australia, that their House of Representatives is just about as unrepresentative as our House of Commons.

The second difference, which follows from the first, is in the counting. This is called 'quota counting', and reading about how it works is like learning to ride a bicycle. Once you've got it, you never fall off again. But it takes perseverance.

Counting the super-vote: the broad outline

The first step is natural: the votes are added up. The Returning Officer will be in a counting-hall just like the ones that have become so familiar in TV General Election reports. The piles of votes will be visible on the long rows of tables, with the counting clerks standing, or sitting, by them and the party agents wandering round the hall. Say the number of votes cast in Beckenham-Croydon is announced as 213,993, the October 1974 total. Seventeen candidates have taken part (there were fifteen from the main parties in October 1974, plus two fringe candidates) and there are five seats to fill.

The second step is also natural. The votes are sorted according to first preferences. Your super-vote will be in the pile belonging to the candidate against whose name you wrote '1' on the ballot paper.

If the same candidates received the same number of votes as they did in October 1974, the sheet would look as shown opposite.

The third step does not come quite so naturally. The Returning Officer has to work out a *quota* of votes — that is, just how many votes each of the five winning candidates must have if he or she is to be declared a winner. Since it is a

Croydon-Beckenham; seats:5; candidates:17
Total votes cast: 213,993

Conservatives

Clark, W.G.	25,703	
Moore, J.E.M.	20,390	
Goodhart, P.C.	19,798	
Weatherill, B.B.	17,938	
Taylor, R.G.	16,035	Total 99,864

Labour

Winnick, D.	20,226	
Simpson, D.	15,787	
Boden, S.J.	14,556	
Sharp, N.J.	11,140	
Keene, D.W.	7,203	Total 68,912

Liberal

Nunneley, D.	11,514	
Mitchell, G.D.	10,578	
Maxwell, I.H.	7,834	
Streeter, P.T.	7,228	
Pitt, W.H.	6,563	Total 43,717

Other

Holland, P. (National Front)	1,049
Stringer, W. (Independent British Nationalist)	451

fair-shares system, this quota must be the same for each candidate, with the lowest possible number of votes left over, or 'wasted'.

The formula used in super-vote counts for establishing the quota is: first divide the number of votes cast by the number of seats to be filled, plus one. That comes to 213,993 divided by 6 = 35,665. But if every candidate received just that many votes you would of course have elected six MPs instead of five. So the quota is increased by one — and becomes 35,666. The full reasoning behind this formula is explained later: the essential principle is that it produces the lowest number of votes necessary to elect each of five candidates, with the smallest number of votes wasted.

The fourth step is easy: you look down the list to see if any of the candidates has enough first-preference votes to make up the quota. The list above shows that in this particular election not one of the candidates can make it at this stage.

The ice-tray has many cubes with too little water in them; none is full. The Returning Officer has to make some transfers.

The fifth step follows perfectly logically. The votes of the hopeless cases are transferred. On the list above you would take Stringer first, then Holland, then Pitt, Keene, and Streeter. The votes of each would be transferred in turn. They would whizz across to the piles of other candidates according to the 2 marks written on them. You might have voted 1 for Pitt and 2 for Nunneley; your super-vote goes up to help Nunneley. Or it might be 1 for Keene, 2 for Simpson — up goes the super-vote. Each time a transfer is made the pile of those who receive the second-choice votes grows a little larger. The ice-tray cubes are filling up. As soon as someone has the quota of 35,666 votes he or she is declared elected.

This avoids the wastage of votes cast for hopeless or losing candidates. But what about the wastage that might occur when *too many* votes are cast for a popular candidate? Say Clark had received 45,000 votes — 10,000 more than the quota. As a popular Tory he might have done so, at the expense of less-popular colleagues. Or say some of the transfers from losing candidates put a leader over the top. What then?

The answer is that the Returning Officer transfers the extra votes to whichever candidates the voter has indicated. You might have voted for Clark on first preference, and he might have too many votes. Your super-vote will then move to help someone else — just who, depends on what you wrote on the ballot paper.

But, people rightly ask, how is it decided which of the votes in Clark's pile of votes are surplus? Which should move across? Votes are not really drops of water moving across to ice cubes; they may be different from one another. Your second choice may not be the same as that of other Clark supporters.

In fact your super-vote is given as fair a chance to move across to another pile as every other super-vote. This is done either by taking the last ('surplus') votes put on the pile, or by taking an arithmetical proportion of the second choices of all of Clark's voters. The two methods are explained in greater detail below.

And so the transfers are made, one at a time. Each time the pile of votes of a certain loser is eliminated the second or third or later choices of the people who voted for that loser get the benefit. Similarly, the surplus votes of a winner are spread about. This process goes on until five candidates each have 35,666 votes by their names — made up of some first preferences for each of them, with usually some second, third or later preferences added on. This means that 5 times 35,666 votes, or 178,330 of the 213,993 were 'useful'.

There will be 35,663 votes over — and this 16.7 per cent of the vote will, alas, be wasted. But it is a great improvement on the wastage of 140,759 votes, or 65.7 per cent of those cast in the October 1974 election in the five separate X-vote seats taken to make up our imaginary maxi-constituency. This is a real figure, taken from the 1974 results. There were about 114,000 votes cast for Labour, Liberal, or fringe losing candidates, and a surplus of 26,630 votes cast for Conservatives who could have won without them.

Counting the super-vote: some details
The militant democrat does not need to know more about the super-vote count than has been set out in the above description. But for those who want to know, the two sets of further details promised above are as follows:

The quota
The idea is that at the end of the counting the piles of votes will be of more or less equal size, just as the ice cubes will all be full. So to work out a quota you ask just how many votes will be in each victor's pile at the end of the count if each one is to be of equal size.

There is a trap here. You might think, 'That is easy; just divide the total number of votes cast by the number of seats to be filled'. Well you *could* do it that way, and when the system was first invented that is the way it was proposed. But consider: if there was just one candidate in a single-member constituency, and you divided by one to get the quota, you would be saying that he or she needed all the votes to win! In fact in a race between two candidates just half the votes plus one would be enough. Work it out: if there were a hundred votes shared between two candidates, fifty-one would be the lowest number necessary to win. And forty-nine would be the lowest possible number of 'wasted' votes.

If the constituency had to return two members, and there were three candidates (the least you would need for a contest in this case), then the lowest number that each of the two winners would need would be one third of the total vote plus one. The arithmetic proves the point. Say there are 99 votes cast (to make the division easy). Then if you divide the number of votes cast by the number of seats to be filled you get 49½. So two of the candidates would have to get 49½ votes each, and the third none. This is clearly wrong. Very well, divide by three — that is, one more than the number of seats to be filled. Then each candidate gets thirty-three votes — clearly a tie and wrong again. So make the quota just one more — 34. Then the least the two winners would need would be thirty-four votes each, while the most the loser could have would be thirty-one. The wasted vote would be down to just under one-third of the total.

And so it goes on. In a three-seat constituency, just one more than a quarter of the votes would be enough to win. That is, if there were a hundred votes cast, the least that each of the three winners would need would be twenty-six votes each, while the waste would be down to twenty-two votes.

The technical name for this simple calculation is the 'Droop quota', after its inventor, a Dutchman called H.R. Droop. It is fair game for those who want to use the chance to mock a funny foreign name as a means of argument; but once the militant democrat has heard the joke a few times he can continue.

The Droop quota can be expressed as a formula:

(Total number of votes) ÷ (Number of seats + 1) + 1 = Droop quota

So a constituency represented by five MPs for whom 960 votes are cast would have a Droop quota of 161. How? Divide the total number of votes (960) by the number of seats plus one (6) to get the answer, 160. Add one. Answer 161. If each of the five winners landed up with 161 votes in his or her pile that would be 805 votes used and 155 votes, or less than 17 per cent, wasted. Thus the merit of the Droop quota is that by making sure that each candidate wins with the smallest possible number of votes, the wastage is kept to a minimum.

If you wish, try the little test given in the British government's Northern Ireland pamphlet. Assume there are twenty-four children voting for three prefects. The answer — the Droop quota in their case — is given at the end of this chapter.

The transfers

The transfer of the votes of the candidate who has least votes is easy enough to carry out. In Northern Ireland the ballot papers themselves are physically re-sorted and shifted over to the candidates on which the second or third or later preferences are marked.

But the transfer of the surplus votes of a candidate who has too many is not quite so simple. How do you decide which votes are to be moved? How do you decide which are to be super-votes?

There are several ways. One is to take the surplus votes from the most popular pile at random, and distribute them to the other candidates. This might be fair, on the ground that a random sample of opinion is usually a fair sample. Another more acceptable way is in fact used in the Republic of Ireland.

All the votes of the candidate with the votes to spare are re-sorted into little piles according to the '2' preferences on them. Some Returning Officers have a big bank of pigeon-holes ready for this re-sorting. Now the second choices of the supporters of that overpopular candidate can be seen, physically. Some of these second preference votes are then taken from each pile and sent along to the candidates indicated by the 2 marks on them. Which? The last to have been put in the pigeon-holes. How many? A fair share taken from each pigeon-hole until the unnecessary extra votes are used up. If the favourite had twice as many votes as he needed to reach his quota then half the votes would be taken from each second-preference pile and moved according to the voter's written instruction. The other half is enough for the quota. If the favourite had a third too many votes, then a third of the votes in each pigeon-hole would be transferred — and so on.

For some people even this is not certain enough to produce a fair result. The Northern Ireland Office pamphlet explains:

'Suppose the quota is 1,000 votes and candidate A gets 1,500

votes in the first count. That means 500 of his votes, a third of
his total, are to be re-distributed as surplus. In the counting
system used in the 1920s, the 1,500 ballot papers were
examined to find out the proportion of second preferences for
the other candidates, and then 500 ballot papers were taken at
random to reflect that pattern, and distributed among the
other candidates.' This is something like the Southern Irish
pigeon-hole method.

'Some people said "That's all very well, but how is anyone to
be sure that the 500 papers transferred reflect faithfully the
pattern of later preferences expressed by the 1,500 people who
voted for candidate A? They don't matter now, but they might
become important later in the count." ' In other words every one
of those 1,500 imaginary voters might have a slightly different
order of preference. They have all chosen the same person as
the candidate of their first choice, of course, but they will split
up (and do in actual elections) in different directions for their
second choices, and in different directions yet again for their
third choices, and so on. The super-vote is above all personal.

It was to meet this obligation, says the pamphlet, that the
'senatorial rules' (so called because they are used to elect the
senates of South Africa and both Northern and Southern
Ireland) were introduced to the Northern Ireland general
election.

'What happens is that instead of transferring one-third of
the votes, all the 1,500 votes are transferred at one-third of
their value. This does not mean that your vote is actually
divided up. It is simply a mathematical way of ensuring that
the value of 500 votes is transferred to the candidates to whom
they are due in the proper proportion.'

Say one of the candidates, needing only 200 votes to win, has
300 votes in his or her pile. According to the senatorial
rules, each of those 300 — the lot — will then be inspected for
second preferences. Say they divide up 180 for one of the other
candidates, 120 for another. Then you would say to yourself —
'the number of extra votes was 100 out of 300 or one-third.
Since 180 of them want to go to that other chap over there, he
would have one-third of 180, or 60 votes accredited to him.
And as 120 want that lady there, she shall have one-third of
120, or 40 accredited to her.' In this way the 100 surplus votes
will have been transferred. The same sums will be done all over

again for third or later preferences. The Returning Officer will by this stage be thanking heaven for the modern calculating machines available to him.

The counting method of the super-vote, or single transferable vote, with its painstaking devices to ensure as much fairness as possible at every stage, is as simple, or if you like complicated, as that. When it is all completed the result will be declared in such a way that you can read off just what happened at each stage. The first column will show the names and parties of each candidate, the number of first-preference votes polled by each one, the total vote, and, at the top of the page, the quota.

The second column will show how the votes of, say, the lowest-scoring candidate have been transferred to all the others, with the new totals for each of them alongside. Then if someone is put over the top, the surplus votes (perhaps transferred by the senatorial rules) will be shared out among the others. The next column will show this, and the next one the new totals. It is just like a map of the collective mind of the electorate, on which you can read off just who each group fancies most, just who each candidate's supporters prefer as second best and so on.

There is no point in inventing such a table for the hypothetical maxi-constituency of Beckenham-Croydon. For, while we know the first preferences of those voters in October 1974, we do not really know their second and third and fourth and fifth preferences. They have not been given a chance to express them. All that can be said is that it seems very likely indeed that in a super-vote election in October 1974 the Conservatives would have won two or three seats, Labour one or two, and the Liberals one, for that is what the first-preference totals for each party indicate. But which Conservatives, and which Labour or Liberal representatives, we cannot be sure. The voters of Beckenham-Croydon have not been asked.

More about the super-vote

The super-vote was first suggested by a Danish liberal politician, C.C.G. Andrae, in 1855. Working quite independently, a previously unheard-of London barrister, Thomas Hare, developed the same idea and put it forward a few years later, first in a pamphlet, then in his major work, *The Election of Representatives, Parliamentary and Municipal,* published in 1859.

Hare's idea was to take the whole country as a single constituency. A candidate could then draw votes from every part of it, although the count would start with the votes cast near his home. The purpose was to provide the maximum opportunity for personal representation; parties were of secondary importance. In present-day terms, someone like Screaming Lord Sutch, or Miss Vanessa Redgrave, might find just enough combined support from all parts of Britain to make it to the House of Commons — 60,000 votes would be sufficient. (When Miss Redgrave did stand, in a single-member constituency in Newham in October 1974, she lost her deposit in spite of the backing of the Workers' Revolutionary Party.) This is clearly an extremely democratic proposal, although its most ardent supporter might find it difficult to persuade many people that it would have been practical, even with the electorate of 1½ million that existed in Hare's time, let alone modern electorates of 40 million and more.

Hare's scheme attracted a most powerful and distinguished advocate in John Stuart Mill. His books, *On Liberty* and *Representative Government,* published in 1861, are the foundation of much subsequent thought and argument about the single transferable vote, just as some of the counter-arguments can be found in Walter Bagehot's *The English Constitution,* published in 1867.

'Every member of the House would be the representative of a unanimous constituency' said Mill. His electors would have selected him 'from the whole country; not merely from the assortment of two or three perhaps rotten oranges, which may be the only choice offered to him in his local market'.

Said Bagehot: 'Mr Mill was returned by the electors of Westminster; and they have never, since they had members, done themselves so great an honour. But what did the electors of Westminster know of Mr Mill? What fraction of his mind could be imagined by any percentage of their minds?'

Much of the debate now seems dated; after all the super-vote is no longer advocated on the basis of making the whole country into one constituency. If there are to be three, five, or seven-member constituencies the idea becomes practical, as the Irish, the Australians and others have conclusively demonstrated. It helps to avoid the 'tyranny of the majority' and thus meets Mill half-way, while providing a workable Parliament, allowing Bagehot at least half his case. It allows political parties to develop, yet it gives more personal representation than any other system.

Since Mill and Bagehot wrote, the single transferable vote has become more or less the only system that British intellectual opinion has been willing to consider. Sadly, we have failed to take it up. We are now saddled with a series of transient and not very efficient but nevertheless powerful executives. What has yet to be learned, it seems, is that there is far less of a gulf between a truly representative Parliament and an efficient Cabinet than British politicians like to imagine; for in modern conditions, when few are deferential, you cannot have the efficiency or the strength without the representativeness. Both Mill and Bagehot might be saying different things if they were alive today.

It is possible to test just how representative *and* efficient the super-vote can be, because it has been used in several places over a great many years. Between 1918 and 1945 nine of our University MPs were elected by this method. The Church of England uses it; so do the Royal Arsenal Co-operative Society, the National Union of Students, the National Union of Teachers, and a great many other organisations in electing their committees. The degree of understanding of the single transferable vote in action in Britain is far more widespread than those of its opponents who mutter 'unintelligible' may imagine.

These non-government elections could not be a sufficient guide, of course. Countries using the super-vote are: Australia (for the Senate, since 1949); Tasmania's Lower House; Malta; and of course both the Republic of Ireland and Northern Ireland. The Republic now has more than half a century of experience of electing the governments of a sovereign state by means of the single transferable vote. In the next chapter the way this has worked out is described. Meanwhile, the view of the Irish people is of some interest.

Two attempts to abolish the super-vote have been made in the Republic. The first, in 1959, was in a referendum combined with the election of a President. One of the candidates was of course the late Eamon de Valera, and his party urged Irish voters to support him and reject the single transferable vote, which would be replaced by the British first-past-the-post system. In spite of this patently unfair method of running the referendum, Ireland's voters kept their heads. They voted de Valera in, all right, by a majority of 120,467. But they also voted to keep the single transferable vote, by a majority of 33,667. There was a low poll, and there were many spoiled papers.

In 1968 there was another referendum, on the same proposal to abolish the single transferable vote and replace it with the British method. This time there was no presidential election to complicate the matter. There was a much higher poll, with far fewer spoilt papers — and the majority in favour of keeping the super-vote shot up to 232,400. Once again the people rejected what some of their most popular politicians had urged, no doubt in the full realisation that the motive of those politicians was to make it easier for them to take, retain, and use executive power.

Answer to puzzle on page 120: The Droop quota is $24 \div 4 + 1 = 7$

10 The super-vote, in practice

Successive Irish governments have done their best to diminish the effectiveness of the super-vote, with some success. Their main method has been to reduce the number of representatives chosen by each of the maxi-constituencies. It is not hard to see why this reduces the power of the vote: the table below shows how this power grows as the number of seats per constituency increases.

number of seats per constituency	quota	guaranteed effective vote just over %	maximum wasted vote just under %
2	1/3 + 1	66 2/3	33 1/3
3	1/4 + 1	75	25
4	1/5 + 1	80	20
5	1/6 + 1	83	17
6	1/7 + 1	85 1/2	14 1/2
7	1/8 + 1	87	13

This is how the table is worked out. In the previous chapter the formula for the quota (the number of votes necessary to elect each member for a particular constituency) was: total number of votes cast, divided by one more than the number of seats to be filled, plus one. So in a two-member constituency it would be one-third of the votes, plus one. That means two winners would each be declared when their piles of votes reached one-third plus one — just over two-thirds, or 67 per cent, of the votes being effective. The wastage of votes then becomes just under one-third. The rest of the table is calculated in the same way.

In a single-member constituency, the kind we have, we could keep the maximum wastage down to about 50 per cent if we introduced the alternative vote. In, say, a single-member constituency with 1,000 voters, just 500 votes, plus one more, would be enough for victory. But then 499 votes — almost exactly half — would be wasted. Thus a single-member system must by definition waste more votes than any of the multi-member constituencies in the above table, even if the alternative vote is used; without AV the wastage is much greater.

Yet with the super-vote itself a third of the votes would be wasted if you had constituencies returning only two members. Say there were 999 votes cast. To get the quota you would divide by one more than the number of members to be elected, which is 999 divided by 3 = 333. Then add one, making it 334. Thus the two winners would together take up 668 useful votes, while 331 votes would be wasted. An improvement, but not enough.

The next step almost gets us there. For with three candidates the wasted vote is down to about a quarter of the votes cast — just low enough to meet our yardstick of giving at least three-quarters of the electorate a say in who shall represent it.

Five- or seven-member constituencies would be much more satisfactory. If there are five seats to fill, the possible wasted vote is down to one in six votes, or just under 17 per cent, while with a seven-member constituency it is down to one in eight, or just under 13 per cent.

If you start making constituencies much larger than that the possible wastage of votes is not very greatly diminished. An eleven-member constituency might waste about 9 per cent of the votes — not enough of an improvement to make up for the unwieldiness of so large a voting unit. As Miss Lakeman shows in a graph on page 128 of *How Democracies Vote*, the added chance of accurate representation with constituencies returning more than about five or seven members is hardly worth the added trouble and confusion that would be created.

In Northern Ireland the average constituency size is between six and seven. Going back to three members for a large number of constituencies as the Irish Republic has done reduces the fairness of the system. For the large parties are unduly favoured by smaller constituencies. In a three-seat constituency a quarter of the votes might be wasted since each of the three members is elected on a quota of about a quarter of the votes. This also means that half the votes (two quarters) elect two members, which is two-thirds of the members. Spread across the country this could mean that a large party polling 50 per cent of the votes could take 66 per cent of the seats in Parliament.

Now look at how the number of three-member constituencies in Ireland has increased over the years:

number of constituencies	number of each size in terms of seats							total number of seats	average seats per constituency
Year	9	8	7	6	5	4	3		
1920 28	—	2	1	2	4	16	3	128	4.6
1923 30	1	3	5	—	9	4	8	153	5.1
1935 34	—	—	3	—	8	8	15	138	4.1
1947 40	—	—	—	—	9	9	22	147	3.7
1959 39	—	—	—	—	9	9	21	144	3.7
1961 38	—	—	—	—	9	12	17	144	3.8
1969 42	—	—	—	—	2	14	26	144	3.4

In short, the proportion of members elected in three-seat constituencies rose from 7 per cent in 1920 to 54 per cent in 1969.

Of course a large party can also do fairly well in a four-member constituency, where it can win half the seats with four out of ten of the votes. The quota is just over 20 per cent of the votes. Two members of the same party can win if between them they attract 40 per cent of the votes. But two seats is half the number going. If a party is strong, but not too sure of its strength, in certain areas four-member constituencies will be preferred to three-member constituencies. The table shows how, after a preliminary fall in 1920, the number of four-seat constituencies rose steadily between 1923 and 1969.

Before the British reader recoils from all this in a fit of piety it should be remembered that in a British general election it is not only possible but actually happens that not half but *all* the seats in many countries are won on four out of ten or less of the votes cast. Measured on this scale the British X-vote in its contemporary form is at least twice as unfair as the super-vote in its peculiar Irish form.

The first-preference debate
According to Dr Garret FitzGerald, Minister for Foreign Affairs for the Republic of Ireland, in a foreword to *Republic of Ireland — The General Elections of 1969 and 1973* by James Knight and Nicolas Baxter-Moore, the bonus can be even bigger than the above arithmetic suggests. For a party winning say 47 per cent of *first preference* votes can usually bank on enough later preferences to give it more than half the total vote

— enough to give it two of the three members in a three-member constituency. In other words with three-member constituencies two-thirds of the seats can be won by a party that attracted *just under half* the first-preference votes.

'This feature of the STV multi-seat electoral system first became apparent in the 1969 redistribution in the Republic of Ireland', says Dr FitzGerald. 'It was the view of the Opposition at that time that by the division of the west and north of the country into three-seat constituencies and most of Dublin into four-seat constituencies that redistribution secured for the Government of the day five or six more seats than they would otherwise have obtained — increasing the normal small "bonus" of seats for the largest party from about 2½ per cent to 6 per cent.'

But is Dr FitzGerald right to base his calculations on first-preference votes? If he is wrong he is not alone — many people judge the efficiency of the Irish version of the super-vote system by relating what happens in terms of seats to votes counted according to first preferences. It could be said, as Dr FitzGerald acknowledges, that this is an imperfect indicator. For the essence of the super-vote system is that it gives people a chance to show their first, second and later preferences for individuals or factions, whatever the official parties may wish.

It is true that in practice in the majority of elections nearly all the successful candidates are the ones with the most first-preference votes. The catch is the 'nearly'; there is often someone put over the top by second and later preferences. The Irish voters can be very choosy. Popular candidates often win far more first preferences than they need, and when their extra votes are transferred to others they sometimes go to candidates of other parties. For example, in the 1973 general election in Ireland, the Prime Minister, Jack Lynch, attracted 12,427 votes for himself and his party, Fianna Fail, in the constituency of Cork City North West. But the quota of votes needed to win was only 6,763. So no fewer than 5,664 surplus votes were available to share out among other candidates according to the *second* preferences marked on Mr Lynch's voting papers. Of course most of these — 4,501 in fact — went to his Fianna Fail running-mate, helping that fortunate candidate right over the top into a surplus of his own. But 1,163 of Mr Lynch's votes went on transfer to candidates of other parties, just as did his running-mate's own surplus of 429 votes.

Thus if you count second and third preferences alone in this particular constituency it is seen that some 1,600 votes, or just over a tenth of the total Fianna Fail first-preference vote of 15,118, went to candidates of other parties. Some of these transferred votes actually counted towards the election of the opposition Fine Gael candidate.

What happened in that case, it is clear, was that some opposition voters in Cork City North West were attracted to Mr Lynch personally, but not to his party. They gave him their first preference, but reverted to their own party after that. This kind of thing happens in many constituencies in every Irish election, although not necessarily on the same scale as in a constituency with a battling Prime Minister standing as one of the candidates.

Another reason why first-preference votes in Ireland are not a precise guide to the strength of feeling about *parties* is that some Irish voters would rather have a local man of a party they do not support than a 'foreigner' representing their own party. Carpet-bagging is bad politics in much of Ireland; Dr FitzGerald refers to the 'tendency for a proportion of votes, when transferred, to pass across party lines to opposing candidates from the same part of the constituency. This tendency is most marked in constituencies comprising all or part of two counties, where strong county loyalties come into play within each part of the constituency.' A final, technical reason why first preferences can be misleading is that small parties that are certain losers appear as first preferences in the result sheets even though votes are quickly transferred away from them in the count.

It does seem reasonable to criticise the Irish version of the super-vote on the ground that there are too many three- and four-member constituencies. It does not seem so reasonable to criticise it on the basis of a relationship between first-preference votes cast and seats won, although many people do.

The Times, in a leading article of 17 June 1975, followed some Irish commentators in making judgements based on first preference voting. 'The Irish experience in the last three elections is not reassuring', it said. 'In 1965 Fianna Fail won 50.3 per cent of the seats on 47.7 per cent of the first preference votes; in 1969 they lost the election in the country, with their votes falling to 45.7 per cent against the combined Opposition vote of 51.1 per cent, but actually increased their share of seats to 51.7 per cent.

'In 1973 Fianna Fail improved their share of the poll — to 46.2 per cent — and reduced the Opposition first preference lead... to 2.6 per cent — but their share of seats fell to 47.5 per cent, so they lost power. For two elections the Irish system produced a Fianna Fail majority on a minority vote, and at the third election produced a Fine Gael-Labour majority on a minority vote.'

Was *The Times* fair? The 1965 result was the product of a distorted version of the single transferable vote in which a third of the representatives were elected in four-member constituencies and more than a third were returned in three-member constituencies. This much has to be said against the Irish version of the system. Yet even if that is accepted and the use of first-preference votes is taken as one standard of judgement, the Fianna Fail government that in 1965 won 50.3 per cent of the seats on 47.7 per cent of those '1' votes was more representative than most British governments. *The Times* commented: 'At all events the Irish system is not a truly proportional system, and will therefore produce somewhat disproportionate results, though not nearly as disproportionate as the present [British] system or as the alternative vote.'

Of course if you count the transfers of second, third and later preferences Fianna Fail had much more reason to justify its forming the government in 1965.

But what about the elections of 1969 and 1973? Were not those results anomalous — possibly just as anomalous as some of the British results criticised in Chapter 1? The answer is, yes if you ignore second and later preferences — and no if you take them into account.

In 1969 the Irish Labour Party stated that it was not interested in a coalition after that year's election. Since Labour in Ireland is the smallest of the three parties (roughly equivalent in degree of support to our Liberals) this might not have mattered in a winner-take-all election, but it did in Ireland. For many Labour voters simply marked preferences for Labour candidates and left it at that. They did not mark later preferences, and so their votes became non-transferable. They voluntarily gave up the use of the super-vote. In the report on the 1969 and 1973 Irish elections quoted above, James Knight calculates that seven of eleven seats won by Fianna Fail in 1969 might have fallen if Labour voters had marked Fine Gael candidates as second preferences, and vice versa. This is because in those cases the number of non-transferable votes was more than the margin by which the Fianna Fail candidate finally reached their quotas and were declared elected.

A British equivalent would be a super-vote election in which the Liberal Party announced that its voters should vote for Liberals only by expressing preferences for Liberals 1,2,3 and then stopping. In a constituency in which Liberals and Labour together outnumbered the Conservatives, the Conservatives might yet win more than their share of seats if the Liberal voters followed such short-sighted advice and refused to mark any preferences for other than Liberal candidates. Their votes would fall out of the counting and they could not help to put any Labour candidates over the top, if that was their desire. Nor could they help Conservatives, if that was what they wanted to do.

The point was proved in the 1973 Irish general election. On that occasion Fine Gael and Labour fought as a team, willing to form a coalition after the voting was over. Each party asked supporters to mark their later preferences for their coalition partner's candidates. This worked very well. Of the sixteen constituencies in which seats changed hands, half were coalition gains from the then government. In six of these eight constituencies the coalition pact could be shown by clear arithmetic to be the cause of victory. This showed a consensus choice of coalition by a large number of votes.

It might be said that all this proves is that Irish voters are just as willing to be fodder for political parties as voters in any other country. Of course this is true. What is also true, and just as plain from the clear and minutely specific records of transfers of first, second, third, fourth and fifth preferences in every Irish constituency in every election for half a century, is that at least a large minority of voters takes advantage of the opportunity to distinguish between individual candidates, an opportunity that does not exist to the same extent under other systems.

The super-vote in Northern Ireland
The natural question is, has the single transferable vote helped

or hindered the search for a solution to Ulster's troubles? The answer is, it probably could have helped; certainly it has not hindered.

The super-vote was used in the first general election to the Northern Ireland Parliament that was set up under the Government of Ireland Act 1920. There were six four-member constituencies (one of them Queen's University, Belfast), one constituency returning five members, another returning seven, and two eight-member constituencies.

That election, in May 1921, was in effect a plebiscite on the new political arrangements for the whole of Ireland. The Unionists, not surprisingly, triumphed. Leaving aside the four special Queen's University seats (which also went to the Unionists) they won thirty-six of the remaining forty-eight seats, four more than their proportional share if you count first-preference votes and ignore second and later preferences. The Nationalists won six seats, their exact proportional share, and Sinn Fein also won six seats, four less than the first-preference vote might have suggested.

The result of the subsequent election, in June 1925, was quite different. Excluding uncontested seats and Queen's University, it was as follows:

party	seats in proportion to first-preference votes	seats won	+ or –
Unionists	22	22	—
Independent Unionists	4	4	—
Labour	2	3	+1
Independents	1	1	—
Nationalists	9	9	—
Republicans	2	1	–1

Thus the proportionality between seats won and first-preference votes cast was almost exact. If you count second and later preferences then it can be said of both the 1921 and the 1925 super-vote elections in Ulster that the system produced what it is fundamentally intended to produce: *proportionality between political ideas*. It may have been a seat or two out on parties, if these are related to first-choice votes, but it was more or less exact on the shares of representatives of different political ways of thinking, as seen by the voters.

The 1925 result must have seemed like a threat to the long-term future of the Unionists. They lost eight seats; in the following years they could lose more. If you count the university and uncontested seats they had thirty-two of the fifty-two MPs in that 1925 Parliament. But if they lost only six more seats they would have only half, and the loss of one more would put them in the minority. They had already lost out to Independent Unionists (four seats), and the class-based rather than sectarian Labour party (three seats).

This could have been the start of a multi-party political system for Northern Ireland, one in which sectarian politics might after some years have receded into the background to be replaced by more usual and less dangerous kinds of politicking. The Unionists need not have become the 'natural' and only rulers of the province. Even if they had, differing trends of political thought among Unionists would have been reflected by super-vote results; it would not have been so easy to maintain a rigidity of approach to everyday questions. If the super-vote had been allowed to develop its own potential the political character of Ulster might have been very different from what it is today.

It was not allowed to develop. The Unionists abolished it. The election of 1929 was held on the X-vote system in single-member constituencies, although proportional representation was kept for Queen's University. The effect was dramatic. In 1925 there had been only eight out of forty-eight seats left uncontested, excluding the four university seats. But the X-vote can be very discouraging. In 1929 nearly half the seats — twenty-two out of forty-eight — were uncontested. In the twenty-six that were the subject of contests the fair shares of the previous election melted away.

This was an X-vote election, so the following table can be read without any reservations about first-preference votes. It shows the only choice the voters were given a chance to make. (See overleaf.)

Including University and uncontested seats, the Unionists ended up with thirty-seven out of the fifty-two seats in the provincial parliament, an increase of five over the 1925 result. Five more seats — and yet their share of the votes cast in contested constituencies was down from 55 per cent of first-preference votes in 1925 to 50.7 per cent of X-votes in 1929.

party	seats in proportion to votes	seats won	+ or −
Unionist	13	18	+5
Independent Unionist	4	2	−2
Liberal	2	0	−2
Labour	2	1	−1
Independent	2	0	−2
Nationalist	3	5	+2

From the party's point of view the decision to change to X-voting was obviously advantageous, at least in the short run.

The effect in the long run can be guessed, although since it is to do with might-have-beens it cannot be proved.

For the next forty years the Unionists ruled Northern Ireland in their own way, untroubled by Protestant splinter parties and under no institutional or electoral pressure to make any attempt to reach an understanding with the Catholic minority of the population. In most elections about half the seats were left uncontested; everyone always knew who would form the next government.

If the Protestants and Loyalists had not been channelled by the X-vote system into a monolithic single party some Ulster governments during those long years of one-party administration might have seen the need to bring representatives of the Catholic population into the ruling councils of the province. Perhaps this might have averted some of the internecine strife that followed.

When in 1963-9 the then Prime Minister Captain Terence O'Neill tried a policy of conciliating the minority he found much of his own Unionist Party against him. The 1969 election was, therefore, heavily contested, with one kind of Unionist fighting another kind of Unionist in twenty-two of the constituencies. But the X-vote could not respond to such refinements of political opinion. After the election Captain O'Neill had to resign because those politicians who opposed his policy of conciliation were still too powerful for him — even though the opinion polls showed a large majority wanting him to stay in office.

The history of Northern Ireland after that has little to do with voting systems. No electoral mechanics could in themselves bring peace to the warring factions there. Yet it is instructive to see what did happen after the super-vote was reintroduced by the British Government in 1973, first for local government elections and then for elections to the new Assembly. There was no Republic of Ireland-style dilution; in fact there were no three or four-member constituencies at all. One constituency — Fermanagh and South Tyrone — returned five members; five constituencies returned six members, another five, seven members, and one constituency, South Antrim, returned eight members.

The purpose, according to the British Government's White Paper on its proposed new constitution for Northern Ireland, was to make sure that the Assembly would 'reflect the wishes of the Community as accurately as possible'.

No one can say that the people of Ulster found the system too difficult to understand. There were no uncontested constituencies; small parties appreciated that they had a chance. The Unionist Party was broken up into four groups.

The results seemed like vindication for those who believed that the way to peace in Northern Ireland lay through a sharing of power between the Protestant and Catholic communities. The various Unionists and Loyalists won fifty seats between them, but they were not a united force. The Catholic-based Social Democratic and Labour Party won nineteen seats. The bridge-building Alliance Party, which hoped to attract the support of both Protestants and Catholics, won eight seats. The remaining seat went to the Northern Ireland Labour Party.

In every case the number of seats won was within a seat or two of precise proportionality to first-preference votes. It could be said that up to two-thirds of the voters of the province had supported parties that were willing to accept a government that shared power between Protestant and Catholic-based parties. James Knight, in *Northern Ireland — The Elections of 1973*, offers one possible summary of the results, grouped by political opinion rather than party label.

The White Paper referred to in his table, overleaf, was published in March 1973. It stipulated (a) that the future government of the province should be drawn from all sections of the community — Catholics as well as Protestants — and (b) that there would probably have to be an 'Irish dimension', meaning some political arrangement with the Republic of Ireland.

		votes %	seats %
Loyalist Coalition and Unionists	Anti-White-Paper	35.4	34.6
Official Unionists Ind. Unionist Liberal Alliance NILP	Pro-White-Paper with different degrees of caution	39.3	41.1
SDLP Rep Clubs Nationalists	Emphasis on Irish dimension	25.3	24.3
		100.0	100.0

From the new Assembly it proved possible to meet the first of these conditions. After much bargaining Mr Brian Faulkner became chairman of a new power-sharing executive. Some members were his own brand of Unionist, some came from the Alliance Party and some were from the mainly Catholic Social Democratic and Labour Party.

But — probably because of the second condition — the embryo government was overthrown by extra-Parliamentary action in midsummer 1974. Organised Loyalist workers went on strike and the Faulkner Executive fell. Most commentators seemed to agree at the time that what most aroused the Loyalists' fury was the proposal to set up a 'Council of Ireland' that would bring Dublin and Belfast together. This was regarded by many as a prelude to attempts to unite Ulster with the Republic, something few of the Loyalists could accept.

None of this could fairly be described as a failure of the super-vote. It did unite what passed for moderate opinion in Ulster at the time, but as the table above shows there was no obvious majority in the new assembly for such a thing as the Irish dimension. Opposition to a Council of Ireland was simply too strong for any democratic institution to override. Curiously enough, the hard evidence for this came from an X-vote election!

In the February 1974 general election, the Loyalists campaigned strongly against a Council of Ireland (or, more precisely, against the Anglo-Irish agreement concluded at Sunningdale, Berkshire, in December 1973 in which the Council was a central point). These Loyalists won 51 per cent of the X-vote cast — and eleven of the twelve seats at Westminster.

(This disproportionate X-vote result may also have helped to sour the political atmosphere in Northern Ireland by reviving pure adversary politics and allowing some Loyalists to delude themselves that 11-1 seats meant 11-1 popular support.)

When the British Government, sitting hard on Mr Faulkner's power-sharing Executive, pressed ahead with the terms of the Sunningdale agreement it was trying to do something that large numbers of Ulstermen could not accept. No voting system can make such a policy work if the people will not let it work.

The combined Loyalists did well again in the October 1974, X-vote British election, so they felt that they were in a strong position to win the next super-vote election in their own province. Their chance came in May 1975. An election was held to produce a convention that would draw up proposals for a new constitution, since the Westminster government had given up on the old Assembly after the Ulster Workers' Council strike had destroyed it.

The United Ulster Unionists did extremely well in May 1975. They won forty-six of the seventy-eight seats, four more than they would have on a strictly proportional share of the first-preference votes. Perhaps the parties opposing them would have done better on first preferences if the Republican Clubs, said to be the political wing of the Irish Republican Army, had not instructed their followers to vote for them only, marking no further preferences, and if there had not been a campaign to boycott the poll. Yet the Convention as a whole was a pretty fair reflection of the views of the people of Ulster, in proportion to their political groupings.

It so happens that the majority of the Protestant Loyalists were in a particularly intransigent mood in May 1975 (as indeed were some of their opponents). The United Ulster Unionists had been voted in on a platform that opposed both power sharing and any Irish dimension. A majority of the voters were willing to support this. The electoral system reflected the general view. It could not change it. But if there is a change of mood in years to come, it will be positive only if substantial numbers of Protestants support moderate politicians. The history of Northern Ireland shows that under the X-vote there would be little or no chance of such a loosening-up being reflected in election results. With the super-vote there would be such a chance.

Judging the super-vote

The militant democrat will at this stage be able to work out how
well the super-vote passes the four tests set up in Chapter 4.

1   *Is the super-vote fair?* It is fairer to voters than to political
parties. In the Republic of Ireland, where the system is distorted
by the use of many three-member constituencies, the average
share of votes not credited to any winning candidate when the
counting was over in the last two general elections was about a
fifth of the votes cast. In the three-member seats themselves this
wasted vote was just about a quarter of the total vote.

Thus even in the Republic of Ireland the super-vote scrapes
through our main test of fairness, which is that the views of at
least three-quarters of the voters must be accurately represented
in Parliament. In Northern Ireland, where the three-seat
constituency is not used, the wasted vote is down to about
one-eighth of the votes cast (14.6 per cent in 1973; 12.3 per cent
in 1975).

Again, in the Republic of Ireland the three- and four-seat
constituencies make life harder for small parties. Even with the
more satisfactory Northern version of the super-vote the larger
parties are slightly favoured; down South the Labour Party has
been consistently under-represented in the Irish Parliament, if
you take the number of seats they have won in proportion to
first-preference votes cast. The beneficiaries have been the two
largest parties, Fine Gael and Fianna Fail. Tiddler parties have
done even worse than Labour. The disproportion of these
results should not be exaggerated. We are talking about a
handful of seats either way — an extreme example would be in
1969 when the Labour Party advised its supporters not to show
preferences for members of other parties, and thus lost return
preferences from its possible allies. It landed up with eighteen
seats, six fewer than its share would be in exact proportion to
first-preference votes. In the North proportionality to first
preferences has so far been much closer.

If the Republic of Ireland version of the super-vote had been
used in the October 1974 election in Britain the Liberal Party
might have won, say, 105 or 110 seats, depending on what voters
did with their later preferences. This is fewer than the 116 seats
due to them in strict proportion to X-votes won, and with the
West German double vote system the Liberals might have been

half a dozen seats better off. But such assertions must be guesswork: if the Liberals were the second choice of most non-Liberal voters they would naturally do far better. And after one or two such elections our whole attitude to voting would probably be far more positive. The effect would be felt by all parties.

Again, even half a dozen or so seats too few would be fairness itself compared to the actual result of the voting in October 1974. Yet should democrats accept such a disproportion?

The answer is that of course they should. The campaign for fair shares for all strands of opinion to be represented in Britain's Parliament would be written off as the work of eccentrics if those who campaigned insisted on proportionality down to the last decimal point. Supporters of proportional representation were once regarded as cranks because of such pernickety arithmetic. The Irish system is a shade too weighted against small or third parties for what is probably the British taste, but that is no obstacle to the introduction of a purer form of the super-vote here. All we need to do is avoid three-member constituencies and keep the number of four-member constituencies down to a small proportion of the total.

2   *Is the super-vote practical?* There cannot be many people who will stand up and say that Britain has been well governed over the past ten years or so; many would assert that the period of poor government has been longer than that. In the Irish Republic, governments of the past few years and more have not acquired such a damning reputation. They have not been as strong as many people in Britain would like them to be in their pursuit of terrorists, but in other areas they have been reasonably efficient, and responsive to the needs of those who have elected them. Long years of Fianna Fail government did not result in a one-party state; in 1973 Fine Gael and Labour between them won one more than half the seats (on 48.8 per cent of the first-preference vote) and the Fine Gael leader, Mr Liam Cosgrave, now leads a national coalition.

This record is all the more remarkable in a country where Republican extremists have for so long been running their own 'army'. Against such a background the stability of democratic government in Ireland is an excellent advertisement for the super-vote. Perhaps the reason is that their Members of

Parliament, no less than their parties, are, by the nature of the way they are elected, better tuned to the thinking of the electorate than recent British governments have been.

3 *Does the super-vote provide personal representation?* It does, and better than any other system. It was to provide personal representation that the single transferable vote was invented, and even with the smaller constituencies used in Southern Ireland it works very well. Detailed studies of the results in both North and South show time and again how first, second and third preferences have moved over to popular candidates — whatever the party — and in each case the voters send an unmistakable message to the politicians. Reporting on the Northern Ireland Assembly election of 1973 Miss Enid Lakeman tells of a former member of the Stormont Parliament who was referred to in his constituency as 'the invisible man' because he was seldom seen there. He was not re-elected and, says Miss Lakeman, 'had to learn the lesson that under STV there is no such thing as a safe seat in the gift of a party'.

Many British politicians will not accept that personal representation is a point strongly in favour of the super-vote. If you have five, or seven, members per constituency, they will say, how can the individual MP look after his or her constituents? The reply is that if the individual MP is forced by the system to spend his waking hours worrying about the number of first-preference votes he will get at the next election, and many of his sleeping hours dreaming about them, he or she will work harder than ever for the constituents.

What is more, Members of Parliament from *all* constituencies, and not just marginals, would feel obliged to be seen in their constituencies, and to respond to calls from individual voters. The Southern Irish MP, working in a culture that expects good service from politicians, and lashed by the fear of losing first-preference votes, many of which are personal votes, probably does more constituency work than his British counterpart. There may be arrangements or understandings that so-and-so will take care of such-and-such a section of the constituency, but there is little chance of regarding any seat as so safe that local work can be neglected. Constituencies are naturally divided up between MPs and future candidates of the same party. Each party does this separately. In the maxi-constituency of Beckenham-Croydon (see Chapter 9) Mr William Clark would still concentrate his energies on what is now Croydon South. He might even have to try a little harder.

Members of the Irish Parliament are far more likely to be local men, originating from or living in their constituencies, than are Westminster MPs. Many are prominent in local government. They probably do more social work, including intervention with local and central government on personal matters, than the average British MP would think was reasonable. They have to — the voters demand it. If there is any danger it is that the MP's role as legislator might be threatened by the amount of time he must spend on his voters, rather than the other way around.

Professor Basil Chubb, of Trinity College, Dublin, describes all this in *Going about persecuting Civil Servants: the Role of the Irish Parliamentary Representative,* printed in *Political Studies,* Volume 11, No 3 (1963). Anyone who asks how the British MP could attend to his surgeries in a multi-member constituency should be directed to it.

4   *Is the super-vote technically sound?* There is no neat answer to the problem of by-elections. In the Republic of Ireland they use the super-vote to elect a single representative to succeed members who retire or die. This is, in effect the alternative vote. It ensures that the successor shall have the support of at least half those who vote, but if the previous representative was a representative of a minority party it could mean a change of party-occupancy of that seat that would not occur in a general election. Another way might be to give the vacant seat to the runner-up in the preceding election; that could be even more unsatisfactory. New members would be co-opted by the party that held the seat; that too is not attractive. Perhaps the Irish way is best; it is better than X-voting, but by no means perfect.

The second part of this question is, is the system easy for the voter to understand? The *voting* part of the super vote certainly is. The Irish seem to have no trouble with it, and if the British can manage to fill in football-pool forms they can certainly manage a 1,2,3,4 choice between politicians.

The *counting* part of the super-vote is not easily mastered unless one is determined to master it. This determination is likely to be restricted to small numbers of voters, and the democrat must ask whether the introduction of a voting system whose precise counting method will be imperfectly understood by the majority of the voters is acceptable. The Irish have come to understand the effect of different ways of voting, as the 1973 elections showed, and perhaps that is enough. But the apparent complexity of counting the super-vote way (and it is more apparent than real) is a mark against it.

The double vote versus the super-vote

Choosing between these two possible voting systems for general elections to our Parliament is not easy. The debate is analysed further in Chapter 12. For elections to other bodies, such as regional assemblies, there is no doubt which system should be chosen, as the next chapter shows.

PART THREE

How — and where — to fight now

11 In Scotland and Wales — and Europe

Scotland needs the super-vote. Wales should have it too. The road ahead for the militant democrat in these regions is straightforward. The proposed new national assemblies should be elected on a system of proportional representation, and the system to be fought for is the single transferable vote. Take these propositions in turn.

The case for some form of fair voting in the Scottish Assembly is cast-iron. It is arguable (although the alert democrat will no longer accept the argument) that simple X-voting in single-member constituencies works well enough when there are just two political parties. First the Tories have a turn, then Labour, then the Tories come back. In each case it could be said that the party supported by the slightly larger number of voters has been given a reasonable chance to govern, for some of the time. There is no need to dispute this often-heard fallacy here, for in Scotland there is no way that it can stand up. Scotland does not have two political parties in the race: it has at least four. And when there are three, four or more parties on the scene then X-voting must by definition produce unfair results. For many, perhaps most, representatives, will be voted in by a minority of their constituents.

Chapter 1 showed how indefensible the results of national general elections have turned out to be as the two-party system in Britain has broken down. When you focus in close-up on Scotland it looks even worse.

In October 1974, for example, the Labour Party sent forty-one MPs to Westminster. Their fair share on the basis of votes cast for Labour candidates would have been twenty-five or twenty-six seats. The Scottish National Party attracted enough votes to send twenty-one or twenty-two representatives to the British Parliament; in fact the X-vote gamble allocated only eleven seats to them. The Conservatives, with sixteen seats, were by chance only one or two seats short of their fair share. The Liberals won three seats, half as many as was their due.

A table of percentages of votes won shows how Scotland's

four-party system had developed by October 1974:

party	votes won %	Scottish seats won %
Labour	36.3	57.7
Scottish Nationalists	30.4	15.5
Conservatives	24.7	22.5
Liberals	8.3	4.2
Others	0.3	—

As for the wasted vote (explained in Chapter 10) a minority of Scottish voters helped to elect their seventy-one MPs. The majority might as well have gone to the cinema as made the trip to the polling booth: they either voted for losing candidates, or their votes were surplus to the requirements of the winners.

If the Scottish Assembly was to be elected on the same principles as the ones that produced the above results, the Scottish Labour Party, with just about a third of the vote, would be in a dominant position, with more than half the seats under its control. Of its forty-one MPs sent to Westminster in October 1974, only twelve were elected by an overall majority of those who voted in their constituencies. The other twenty-nine were all minority MPs, and six of them won on less than 40 per cent of the votes.

Such disproportion would surely devalue the Assembly in the eyes of most of the two-thirds of the Scottish electorate that had voted against the party. Fair-minded Labour supporters would no doubt feel the same way. Yet it is always tempting for a party that thinks it will benefit from a particular system to come out in its favour. This presumably explains the British Labour government's decision, first announced in a White Paper in September 1974, that membership of the new assembly 'will be on the same system as membership of the United Kingdom Parliament, that is, a single member elected for a geographical area. This is simple to operate, easily understood by the public and provides for the clear and direct accountability of the elected representative to his constituents.'

The benefit to the Labour Party would be doubled, assuming their support remained at least at the October 1974 level, if a further proposed device was used. For the new assembly could have, say, twice as many members as are sent to Westminster — 142 Assemblymen and women. In the long run a boundary commission could draw up lines for the 142 new constituencies. Since this would take time, Labour has had the bright idea that in the first X-vote election to the new assembly each existing Parliamentary constituency should return two representatives. Each voter would have two votes.

Of course this would double the unfairness. For most Labour voters will naturally vote for the two Labour candidates in their constituencies, while most Conservatives will vote Tory twice and so on. It has always happened this way where the block vote has been used; the most obvious example is local council elections. The result would be disproportion multiplied by two. There is no excuse that the honest democrat could accept for such a transparent electoral machination even if it were argued that it was to be used just once only, until the new constituency boundaries were drawn.

But fairness is not the only reason why the new assembly should be elected on a proportional system. Scotland is in a state of political turmoil. The divisions between socialists and non-socialists run deep. So do the criss-crossing divisions between nationalists and those who wish to maintain the United Kingdom in its old form. Most Scots want change, but there is no single kind of change that an overwhelming and convincing majority of Scots have yet agreed on — and there is certainly no such change in the offing that would provide for the protection of minorities.

If there is to be radical change, democracy in Scotland will only survive the accompanying shocks if it is change that commands a wide measure of agreement. A socialist-minded assembly based on Labour's third of the votes could not command such acquiescence in its policies. The same would apply to Tories who tried a tough true-blue policy. A nationalist-dominated assembly that campaigned strongly for Scottish independence would be just as disruptive if it was the product of an electoral fluke.

Such a fluke is quite easy to imagine. The Scottish National Party could win a majority of the seats in a future Assembly election if it increased its share of the vote to, say, between 37 and 40 per cent. This is not an impossible target: the SNP attracted 11.4 per cent of the Scottish vote in 1970, 21.9 per cent in February 1974 and 30.4 per cent in October 1974. After the 1975 referendum on whether Britain should remain a member of the European Economic Community many people in London thought that the Scottish Nationalist tide was receding, because the party had campaigned for a 'No' vote and Scotland had voted 'Yes'. But then half the Scottish Labour Party had also campaigned for a 'No' vote, and the SNP itself was divided on the issue.

Professor Richard Rose, of the University of Strathclyde, has calculated, in his paper *The Future of Scottish Politics*, that if the October 1974 results are taken as a base, then the Scottish National Party would need only a 5 per cent swing to its side from the leading party in each Scottish constituency to deny any party in the Assembly, itself included, an absolute majority of seats. With an 8 per cent swing the Scottish Nationalists would gain a comfortable majority of seats.

How likely is a 5 or 8 per cent swing to the SNP at the next Scottish ballot? Professor Rose points out that between 1970 and February 1974 the overall swing from Labour to the SNP was 9.3 per cent, although this fell to 7.2 per cent in October 1974. The swing to the SNP from the Conservatives was about 8 per cent in both February and October 1974. It is perfectly possible, then, that if the X-vote system is used for the Scottish Assembly the Nationalists could quickly find themselves in control of it.

The party would then presumably carry out its own declared policy, which would be to demand independence for Scotland, and Scottish ownership of and control over 'Scottish oil' (North Sea oil). Never mind the embarrassment for the Westminster government that this would cause; Scotland itself would be as bitterly torn apart by such a demand from a party elected to power on a minority of votes as it would be if red Clydeside tried to run the country on a similarly narrow foundation, or if the Edinburgh Tories attempted to enforce their own ideology.

Let there be no mistake about the principle involved here. If a large majority of Scots want a socialist state, or an independent state, and vote accordingly, then an assembly elected by proportional representation would make this unmistakably plain. The demands would be genuine and difficult to resist, whatever outsiders may have to say about the mixed economy, or the unity of the kingdom. Under any electoral system, such political strength could not be ignored.

But the truth is that there is no such unanimity in Scotland. The only stable and progressive form of government that is possible there is one that forces the various parties to it to compromise. Professor Rose says that the alternatives are 'a Labour-Conservative coalition in defence of the Union; a Labour-SNP coalition advocating radical economic policies; or an SNP-Conservative coalition opposed to socialism'. This may seem unrealistic to inhabitants of a United Kingdom accustomed to ping-pong politics; elsewhere, and especially in continental Western Europe, it is the stuff of democracy. A genuinely representative Scottish Assembly might over time produce a pattern of shifting coalitions, depending on what was being argued about.

When these arguments are set out in this way the temptations to the Labour left, or the less canny of the Nationalists, or some of the Thatcher Tories to support the X-vote must be very powerful. Surely it is better to gamble on victory (even if it is a shallow one based on a minority of the votes) than to saddle oneself with the almost insuperable task of winning over an overall majority of the Scottish electorate to a particular point of view? The answer, in a country as divided as Scotland today, must be that if you do not create that genuine popular majority the policy, whatever it is, is bound to fail.

The protection of minorities is also important. The Report of the Royal Commission on the Constitution (the Kilbrandon Report) which was published in October 1973 says: 'An overriding requirement for the regional assemblies would, in our view, be to ensure the proper representation of minorities, and it would be no bad thing for a regional government to have to pay regard, in the formulation of its policies, and in its administration, to the views of the minority parties, or indeed to be obliged to seek a consensus with them.' (Paragraph 787.)

In the memorandum of dissent to this report, by Lord Crowther-Hunt and Professor A.T. Peacock, it is stated (paragraph 135) that: 'In any democracy there is a crucial problem about the rights of minorities. The minorities in this context are not only racial or religious — though these may be the most lasting and the most important. But on some issues the minority may be trade unionists or employers or professional people ... in fact any group of people with common interests is likely to find itself a minority at some time or other.

'And the essence of the problem here is that if the vital interests of minorities are overridden or neglected by an insensitive majority the essential basis of consensus in society will be eroded and minorities will feel forced to take to the streets in often violent direct action....'

Government by a series of purpose-built coalitions is one way of making certain that all sections of the community participate in the making of at least some of the decisions. But is this 'strong' government?

Those who oppose proportional representation because they persist with the delusion that only a British system produces 'strong government' need not concern themselves about the matter when it comes to Scotland. The Kilbrandon Report answers the point thus: 'The objection that it tends not to give any one party a majority in the assembly would be less substantial when the government was concerned with responsibilities in the domestic field only than would be the case with a government having to take important decisions on major questions of policy, for example in the fields of defence, foreign affairs and management of the economy, all of which subjects would necessarily be reserved to the United Kingdom Parliament and Government.' (Paragraph 787.)

Scottish Nationalists may protest at this. They want an independent Scotland, with its own Parliament controlling foreign affairs and the economy — and presumably defence. Since seven out of nine member countries of the European Economic Community manage these aspects of government quite well without brute majority systems like the British one they can rest assured. The only point that needs emphasising here is that for everyone who is thinking of Scotland as a self-governing country rather than a future independent state — and this applies to all parties except the Nationalists — the 'strong government' argument, for all its speciousness, simply does not arise.

In fact the Kilbrandon Commission specifies that its recommendation for proportional representation applies only to regional assemblies: 'we are not here concerned with elections to the United Kingdom Parliament', it says. (Paragraph 788.)

The super-vote for Scotland

The militant democrat can enjoy the luxury, in Scotland, of

forgetting about endless disputes between the merits of different fair systems of voting. It is true that the British government might argue that all regional assemblies should have the same voting system as Westminster, and that if there is to be a change in the method of election to the Westminster Parliament then perhaps Scotland should get along with X-voting until the new national system is decided. This is so obviously a delaying tactic that there need not be much time spent on it; it might have some validity if there were a declared intention to introduce a specific new electoral reform for all of the United Kingdom at a known date, but not otherwise. Militant anti-democrats do not accept this kind of argument when they espouse their own various causes; militant democrats ought to be just as hard-headed.

The system that has always been proposed for Scotland is the single transferable vote. Its logic appeals to the clear-thinking Scottish mind. It was used in four elections, between 1919 and 1928, to elect the 987 members of no fewer than thirty-eight separate Scottish Education Authorities. It is used in another part of the United Kingdom, Northern Ireland, and Scots who are conscious of their own sectarian divisions will readily understand its value.

In the Kilbrandon Report it is stated categorically in paragraph 788 that 'We, therefore, favour the single transferable vote system, as the one most likely to give parties representation in proportion to their support in the region.' The alternative vote was considered and rejected, although it could be considered for 'areas of sparse population where constituencies would otherwise be unduly large'.

The Crowther-Hunt minority report, which disagrees with the majority about most other matters, concurs: 'They will be elected on the single transferable vote system of proportional representation. This is so we can be sure that minorities will be fully represented — which is particularly important in those areas where recent voting patterns suggest one party could be in a "perpetual" majority ....' (Paragraph 249.)

The Scottish Liberals, like their counterparts elsewhere, are committed by their party policy to the super-vote for Scotland. This is brave of them, for their share of the vote is usually so low that the natural slight bias towards larger parties in even the fairest of single transferable vote systems is likely to work against them. After a few elections they could be squeezed out, leaving the field to Labour, the Conservatives, and the Nationalists.

Many senior Scottish Conservatives, alarmed at the dwindling support for their party in Scotland, have also come out in favour of the super-vote. Charles Findlay, vice-chairman of the Kinross and West Perthshire Conservative Association, has produced a schedule of twenty-six possible multi-member constituencies for the election of a Scottish Assembly by the super-vote. The existing district and regional boundaries are used as a base. The average number of members per constituency is 5.5 — enough to ensure maximum fairness. Malcolm Rifkind, the Tory member for Edinburgh Pentlands, and chairman of a committee on devolution, also favours STV. But other Scottish Tories — and Mrs Thatcher — have been cool to the idea, or opposed it outright.

The Electoral Reform Society in Scotland has drawn its own suggested map, published in a pamphlet in September 1975. It envisages an assembly of two hundred members, returned by thirty-nine constituencies, an average of just on five members per constituency. Privately, a number of moderate-minded Labour MPs from Scotland have also discussed the possibility of STV for the Scottish Assembly.

With all this support for one particular system building up, the task of the democrat in Scotland is to throw his weight behind that system.

Wales

The pressure for an elected assembly in Wales has been less strong than in Scotland. Plaid Cymru is nothing like so successful a party as the SNP. It attracted 11.5 per cent of the Welsh vote in 1970, and just under 11 per cent in the two 1974 general elections. On the other hand the Labour Party is still without doubt the 'natural governing party' of the Principality. Its share of the votes cast in the last three elections was: 1970, 51.6; February 1974, 46.8; October 1974, 49.5.

Perhaps this is what Lord Crowther-Hunt and Professor Peacock had in mind when they referred in paragraph 249 of their dissenting report to 'areas where recent voting patterns suggest one party could be in a "perpetual" majority'. There is no reason why the Welsh should not have a 'perpetual' Labour majority in their assembly, if that is what most of them want. But the super-vote would protect minorities in such an assembly

— and it would go one better than that.

For, as has been seen, this is the method of voting that gives the greatest power of choice to individual voters. Welsh electors need no longer accept whichever Labour candidate their local party committees select for them (although they could if they wished to). They would be marking their first preferences and second preferences among the various Labour candidates. The result sheets would be remorseless: everyone in every constituency would know just which candidate, and which shade of party opinion, had the most first-preference votes and which had the fewest. Every super-vote election has elements of a general election, a party primary, and a plebiscite rolled into one. In an area with a perpetual majority for one party this degree of selectivity should be demanded as of right.

In both Scotland and Wales the important principle is to avoid being too clever. One moment a Labour Minister might argue that both regions could best be kept in Labour hands by retaining the X-vote. Another moment — after an adverse by-election, or a disturbing opinion poll — the same Minister might lose his nerve. He might fear a Nationalist take-over in Scotland, and argue accordingly that for the sake of the unity of the kingdom perhaps proportional representation is not such a bad idea after all. There is no way of avoiding this kind of self-interested judgement, but the alert democrat will always point out, whatever the argument, that the real need is to give the Scottish people an opportunity to decide for themselves what they want. This might mean that one section of opinion in Scotland has to come to terms with another — but only a playground politician could object to that.

The European Parliament

For the militant British democrat, eyes focussed hard on Britain's own internal problems, the primary interest in the possibility of future direct elections to the European Parliament is that it may sharpen the more immediately pressing debate about elections to the Parliament at Westminster.

To say this is not necessarily chauvinistic or short-sighted; it is simply that the need for reform in Britain is too urgent for there to be room for arguments that can be conducted in a more leisurely fashion. (Likewise, in the immediately preceding outline of the case for elections by super-vote to the new regional assemblies in Wales and Scotland, the separate issue — whether there should be a new third tier of government at all — was ignored because it would have led up an unproductive side-track.)

Of course the time may (will?) come when the British Parliament has to legislate on a form of voting for British representatives to be sent to Strasbourg. It may be that when that happens the powers of the European Parliament will be increased, so that the question of who represents us there will be a matter of genuine importance. People who believe passionately in the unification of Western Europe will hope that these two conditions are met as soon as possible, for the one depends upon the other, but the debate about whether the existence of a strongly directly-elected European Parliament would be beneficial is not part of this report.

On the other hand the fact that such a debate is taking place, and is likely to grow in intensity, is of great help to proponents of electoral reform in Britain.

Article 138(3) of the Treaty of Rome, under which the original European Economic Community of Six was created, requires the existing European Parliament to 'draw up proposals for elections by direct universal suffrage in accordance with a uniform procedure in all member states'. That was in 1958, and there have been several false dawns since then.

In 1960 a report by a Belgian member of the Strasbourg parliament, Fernand Dehousse, suggested one method of holding direct elections in every one of the then half-dozen member states. As nothing has been done about it since then, the Dehousse plan can be left where it has lain ever since, 'on the table' at Strasbourg.

In December 1974 the enlarged Community of Nine noted in a communiqué issued after a 'summit' conference in Paris, that 'elections by direct universal suffrage could take place at any time in or after 1978.' The British government was at that time preparing for the referendum on continued membership of the EEC. So it added a note of reservation to that effect. The Danes, too, declined to commit themselves.

Meanwhile a Dutch Socialist MP, Schelto Patijn, produced a fresh proposal for direct elections; this was accepted by the European Parliament in January 1975. It would give the United

Kingdom 67 members in a 355-member parliament, as against its present 36 seats out of 198. This is not strictly in proportion to Britain's share of the population of the community; the Patijn allocations are weighted in favour of the smaller countries. Another scheme, favoured by the Political Affairs Committee of the European Parliament, would provide for 550 members, 116 of whom would represent the United Kingdom.

In the end the choice must be made by both the Council of Ministers — the real power in EEC affairs — and the individual national governments. It is likely that if the Parliament at Strasbourg is to be directly elected the first few elections will be held under different systems in each country, but that some proclamation will be made to the effect that the member governments hope that a uniform system of election can be introduced as soon as possible. It was with this in mind that the Belgian Prime Minister, Mr Tindemans, spent much time in 1975 touring the capitals of Western Europe to prepare a report on direct elections.

At first sight the idea of even trying to produce a single system of election that would be acceptable to the nine member countries of the EEC seems absurd. Britain and France are both wedded to single-member constituencies, although the French use the second ballot to overcome their natural argumentativeness. Ireland, alone, uses the super-vote. West Germany, alone, uses its unique double vote system. The rest all use one form of party list proportional representation or another, with different rules in each country.

A second glance shows that the task may perhaps be less impossible than it seems. Only Britain and France have strictly non-proportional systems, and in France the pressure for change to a proportional system is persistent. In Britain, for purely domestic reasons, the campaign for electoral reform is building up. And the British delegation of thirty-six to Strasbourg, appointed under existing rules by the government from members of the House of Commons and the Lords, is even more disproportionate and unrepresentative than the Parliament from which it is chosen.

Before the referendum of June 1975 the Labour Party declined to send representatives to Strasbourg. Once the 'yes' vote was in, however, the Labour government claimed eighteen of the thirty-six seats for its party, cutting the Liberal Party representation from two down to one (to represent half as many voters as had voted Labour in October 1974!) and trimming the Conservative contingent to enable a lone Scottish Nationalist to have one seat.

No such party-political unfairness would have been possible under direct elections. Lord O'Hagan introduced a bill in the House of Lords in May 1974, providing for single-member constituencies and the alternative vote. This would not have produced proportional representation, but at least the government of the day would not have such overriding power to favour its own party. In July 1975 the Liberal MP Clement Freud tabled a bill providing for the single transferable vote. Both attempts failed.

The choice of a fair proportional system for direct elections to the European Parliament is complicated. The super-vote would not be particularly convenient if there were only thirty-six representatives of the United Kingdom, since natural regions like Northern Ireland would have only two members, while Wales might have to be a single-member constituency using the alternative vote. If there were sixty-seven seats for the United Kingdom, as provided for in the European Parliament's official scheme, these technical difficulties would be much diminished and the standard regions of the country could be the basis for most super-vote constituencies. With 116 seats, which is also a possibility, the problems of constituency size would disappear altogether, although the boundary commissioners would have a lot of work to do.

The West German double vote might be easier to introduce quickly if direct elections to a European Parliament had to be held before the British internal system of voting was itself changed. It would also have the advantage of being easier to tailor to the party list systems used by a majority of member countries. It would certainly guarantee proportional representation for the main British political parties, but British voters would have little choice between individual representatives.

Perhaps this would not seem to matter much in the early years, since only a limited number of people believe in the likely future effectiveness of the Strasbourg Parliament. But if it does become more powerful then one day it might matter very much indeed whether the British Socialist (or Tory, or Liberal) delegation is mainly of one particular leaning or another.

Like all European issues, this one is not Britain's alone to decide. Of course if there are to be direct elections by a different system in each member state then the contrast between these and the fairer elections of all the other countries except France will be instructive. But if there is to be a unified system, then Britain will find it almost impossible to resist the pressure for some proportionality — and that would certainly reflect on the way in which the Westminster Parliament is elected.

The militant democrat must hope that British elections will be conducted under a fairer system long before the date the Europeans have in mind for a uniform system of continental elections, which is some time in the 1980s. But the opportunity is there, in the meantime, to take part in the discussions about those far-off elections as a means of drawing attention to the need for immediate reform here at home.

12 On to Westminster

'We are now at a time when the metal of politics is fluid, is molten', Churchill told the House of Commons on 2 June 1931, when Britain last faced a great depression. 'The various moulds are ready, and we have now, perhaps, a chance in this year or two to decide into which moulds that metal should be guided.'

The decision quickly made itself. Within a few months the National Government was formed. The mould hardened, and hard it stayed for nine years, until Churchill was called upon to lead the wartime coalition. Those nine years were not the most glorious in our history.

Today, once again, the metal of British politics is fluid, Never mind the Celtic fringes: the three national political parties have divided into at least six factions. The left wing of the Labour Party, like its right wing, is itself fragmented. There is little agreement between the free-market and interventionist wings of the Conservative Party. The individualists among the Liberals are under attack from the 'new left' within their own ranks. As if this were not enough, Parliament is itself devalued. Many of the important decisions of government are no longer under its control. This is why so many new groups seek 'direct action' or 'community politics', while at the very top the ring of power (Ministers — Civil Service chiefs — Trade Union leaders — sometimes Chairmen of major companies or nationalised industries) is seldom broken.

Fragmentation
If pure untrammelled proportional representation was to be introduced under these conditions it is possible — no, likely — that the worst fears of those who oppose it would come true. The six factions might become six separate parties; no doubt these would split, and drift apart, and rejoin, and propagate new groups. Absolutely fair shares, as in Holland or Israel, would give every little band its own seat or half-dozen seats in the House of Commons. The Israelis are held together by the necessity to survive: they can manage such a fragmented

Parliament, even though many of their politicians do not like it. The Dutch have generations of experience in arranging compromises among themselves (even today one kind of Dutch Protestant family may be reluctant to have its milk delivered by the dairy of another kind of Dutch Protestant). In its present mood Britain would probably find a Parliament of a hundred opinions unworkable. Those who dread the fissiparous tendencies of unadulterated party list proportional representation would be right to oppose any such thing for Britain.

Fortunately, no such thing is being proposed. None of the present campaigners for electoral reform wants pure party list proportional representation for Britain. The alternative vote (Chapter 6), which is favoured by some, is simply a way of ensuring that individual MPs are elected by at least half those who turn up at the polls in their constituencies; it does not even pretend to provide fair shares in Parliament, let alone fresh opportunities for new small parties. The double vote, as the West Germans have developed it (Chapter 8), discriminates in several important ways against small parties, and not just by means of the 5 per cent hurdle that is quoted by those who say against this system that small parties have once or twice nearly managed to surmount it. Like the Germans, the Irish have so restructured their own fair voting system — the super-vote — that they have gradually shed smaller parties, and thus evolved a two-large-party, one-small-party structure.

In Britain we would probably want the hurdles to be set rather lower at first. There is plenty of room for more liberalisation: no current proposal for electoral reform in this country would make it possible for any new national party to win seats in Parliament unless it could attract more votes than our present Communists, National Front, Workers Revolutionaries and the like put together.

Thus the objection to reform that is based upon the supposed dangers of providing an opportunity for every small fringe party to find a place in Parliament is not really relevant to the debate in Britain.

The same applies to objections based on vague references to collections of foreign countries put together, or to certain individual countries. Italy and Israel are often mentioned in the same breath, but the two countries have different versions of the party list system, different histories, and different tempera-

ments. Italian politics are untidy, and post-war Italian history is
no advertisement for the electoral system used there.
Fortunately, the system is not proposed for Britain, not by
anyone. Nor would proportional representation in any form
have the same political results in Britain as it has in Italy, where
the Catholic Church has held sway over one part of the Italian
voters' minds for so many years, while the Communist Party has
made so much headway in the wake of the Fascist dictatorship.

None of this can be said of Britain; the Italian example would
only be a valid argument against all forms of proportional
representation if it was itself the only practical example of PR in
use. Since PR is the preferred method of election chosen — with
generally excellent results — by most Western European
governments, arguments based on the single outstanding
failure among those governments cannot have any validity save
the strictly limited one of saying that the Italian version of it
does not seem to have saved the Italians from their own peculiar
political and economic malaise.

Choosing a Prime Minister

A serious objection to reform, and one that needs to be
answered, is that the existing party system is a tried, trusted,
and valuable method of gathering together the energies of tens
of thousands of people who wish to take an active part in
political life. The three major national parties — Conservative,
Labour and Liberal — are in themselves valuable instruments
of our democracy, this argument runs. They should not be cast
aside just because for a moment there seem to be more divisions
of opinion within and between them than our system can
absorb. If we encourage the break-up of these parties there is no
telling what strange combinations might come to rule over us.

This is best answered by first following the classic theory in
favour of the majority system a little further. In *Capitalism,
Socialism and Democracy* Joseph A. Schumpeter initially
dismisses proportional representation on the grounds that (a) it
would 'offer opportunities for all sorts of idiosyncracies to assert
themselves' (a point dealt with above), and that (b) 'it may
prevent democracy from producing efficient governments and
thus prove a danger in times of stress', something Schumpeter
might not assert today in face of the evidence of the inefficiency
of the UK government and the obvious efficiency of most the of

PR-elected governments of North-Western Europe. But then Schumpeter adds:

'If acceptance of leadership is the true function of the electorate's vote, the case for proportional representation collapses because its premises are no longer binding. The principle of democracy then merely means that the reins of government should be handed to those who command more support than do any of the competing individuals or teams. And this in turn seems to assure the standing of the majority system within the logic of the democratic method, although we might still condemn it on grounds that lie outside of that logic.'

Schumpeter makes this clear when he goes on to say that the primary function of the vote is to produce government, which really amounts to deciding who shall be Prime Minister. First published in 1942, his notion seems to be extremely up to date thirty or more years later, when television contests between party leaders have become the central feature of general elections.

Who shall be Prime Minister? He who can command most support. But we do not elect our Prime Minister directly (as the French elect their President directly — ensuring, by multiple ballots that he shall be seen to have the support of at least half the votes). Leaving aside the tempting sidetrack of whether we should elect our Prime Ministers in a presidential manner, the British means of demonstrating that you have most support is to command the leadership of your party — and then to make sure that your party wins enough seats in Parliament to guarantee you a majority and thus the occupancy of Number 10 Downing Street. Seats count; the popular vote does not.

In theory our present parties manage this system well. Factions may come and factions may go, but everyone has to find enough common ground to stay inside the party. Left-wingers have nowhere else to turn but to the Labour Party — so the theory runs — while where else could right-wing Tories with a serious appetite for power settle themselves but in the Conservative Party? The majority system makes certain that those at the extreme end of the political spectrum modify their views; if they hive themselves off to splinter parties (the National Front; the Communists) they will get nowhere.

These unifying parties, the conventional argument continues, must themselves shift towards the centre of opinion if they are to win elections. A far-left Labour Party or an extreme-right Tory Party could not win an election, so once again the parties are obliged to be moderate, to avoid politics that repel the floating voter, to stick to the centre. There were little difficulties in 1974 and 1975, this theory goes on, but the natural processes always reassert themselves in time and the two-party system is still the best way of ensuring that our political energies are channelled into a useful direction. National party leaders, from whom our Prime Ministers are chosen, are thus obliged to be men, or women, of moderation; if they are not, they cannot hope to win elections. Introduce a new voting system and you risk destroying all this, with only uncertainty put in its place.

This kind of argument may have *seemed* true a generation or two ago, but it cannot be accepted today. The parties in England are not bringing people of diverse opinions together, they are driving them apart, and they have been doing so during most of the Sixties and Seventies, not just in 1974 and 1975. The system is not making it possible for a plain majority of the people (never mind a minority) to choose a government or a Prime Minister; the matter seems to be open to pure chance. It is based on seats, not the popular vote. Parties, once in power, do move towards the centre after a year or two — but those early years of ideological, unpopular minority rule can be destructive of our political cohesion, damaging to our economy and in the long run a threat to our democracy. Prime Ministers are no longer pillars of moderation or leaders towards national unity; they are becoming prisoners of party factions, or of events, or both. This is true whether you are speaking of Selsdon Conservative or Collectivist Labour governments.

Leadership is still an immensely powerful force in Britain and perhaps we should be grateful for that. Yet our increasingly sophisticated electorate is becoming ever more wary of sham leadership, or leadership that values party unity above the needs of the country. Pure elitism will no longer suffice, whichever party it comes from. It may be desirable that individual party leaders should so symbolise whole political philosophies that elections should constitute a choice of Prime Minister. If so, the choice should be a genuine one. Nobody who cannot call on the proven support of representatives of a true overall majority of the people should become Prime Minister. A PR system can ensure this. It could even go further, acting as a kind of direct election of the Prime Minister, as it does when West Germany chooses its parliament and Chancellor. There is no axe to grind here: which representatives will provide that opportunity for leadership is up to the voters; it does not affect the argument either way.

Permanent coalition?

To this classic objection to reform there is now added an opposite, contradictory argument. Proportional representation, it is said, will result in the stifling imposition of permanent government of the centre (which, incidentally, is precisely what heppened without it in 1931-40, not to mention other more recent periods of our history). A radical socialist policy would be impossible because no Labour government could be formed without the Liberals; a radical Conservative policy would be ruled out because no Conservative government could be formed without the Liberals.

'You cannot trust the bloody Liberals', Mrs Margaret Thatcher is widely believed to have said when approached about proportional representation by some of her Parliamentary colleagues shortly after her accession to leadership of the Tories. The view is shared by many in the Labour Party.

There are three answers to this. One is that it is elitist and anti-democratic to say to the voters 'You may throw the dice for the Montagus and you may spin the wheel for the Capulets, but you shall not have rules that allow you the effective choice of them or anyone else, or a coalition between either clan and anyone else — even if that is what you mostly want'. Another is that single-party rule is perfectly possible under proportional representation. The West Germans have had it, and the Irish. The only need is for one party or another to persuade a majority of the voters to support it. The third answer is that unless voters are given the freedom to choose — even to choose a coalition, if they want it — government will no longer work.

Some will say that this is disingenuous. Everyone knows, such objectors will insist, that the result will be a permanent coalition. But which permanent coalition? Labour politicians fear that the whole movement towards proportional representation is a Conservative plot, designed to keep the left out of power forever. Conservative opponents of electoral reform will assert with an equally convincing air of certainty that the result will be a permanent Lib-Lab coalition; 'permanent social democracy'. Perhaps. But West Germany's PR-elected social democracy is admired by many Conservatives including those close to Sir Keith Joseph and Mrs Margaret Thatcher. Sweden's PR-elected social democracy is often held up as an example by many in the Labour Party, although perhaps not by the very far left. Could it be that for the present, until they find something they prefer, the great majority of British voters want a mixed economy, with generous social benefits paid for by vigorous industry: something that would be labelled social democracy? Could it be that they would quite like to choose between competing parties who may wish to steer this social democracy, this successful modern Western European form of government, left or right as their taste directs them?

Those who say, 'You know very well the answer is yes' might stop there and ask themselves, if that is so, why any obstacle should be placed in the way of the British people having such a government. Anyway, the answer may not be 'yes', or, more likely, it may be 'yes' this year, and something quite different next year, but that is hardly the point. Either the voters must be enabled to choose, or we should cease pretending that ours is a genuine political democracy and get on with the construction of the new corporate state, or the new socialist state, or the new laissez-faire capitalist state, or whatever.

The corporate state
It might reasonably be counter-argued that whichever party is in power, Labour or Conservative, the reality of the economic situation will force the government to seek an understanding with the trade unions and possibly the leaders of industry. The 'corporate state', it is said, is inevitably a product of our failure to solve our economic problems for so many years; no electoral arrangement can do anything about it.

Perhaps. It could be that any non-totalitarian government of Britain in its present economic condition will feel obliged to make deals with the representatives of both managers and producers. There may be no other constructive course; it is impossible to be certain until something different has been proved workable.

What is certain, however, is that if the wheeler-dealing with the trade union bosses and others was conducted by a government that was seen by everyone to represent an absolute majority of the population the balance of power would be changed. It might be the representatives of the people, not the non-representative leaders of some trade unions, or some industries, whose views carried most weight. If there has to be planning, and an incomes policy, or a Social Contract, then at least let the Cabinet approach the negotiating table with the strength of a truly representative Parliament behind it. And if most members of such a Parliament happened to be elected by the voters who did not want planning or an incomes policy — something that might mean confrontation with vested economic interests — then, once again, it would be the power of a genuinely representative institution that would be asserting itself.

Anyhow, the effect of electing our Parliament by some form of fair voting is likely to be so electric that neither of these prognostications need necessarily come true. For what we are seeking through electoral reform is the restoration of the power of Parliament, so that the vast majority of people, including both bosses and trade unionists, come once more to see and accept that the government of the country is in the hands of the elected representatives of the people. In such circumstances it might be hoped that the managers and producers would confine themselves to industrial matters without trying to usurp Parliament's functions in shaping overall domestic and foreign policies. This may be too much to hope for, but it might at least be possible, if there were electoral reform. Without it the prospect on this front is indeed bleak.

'Community politics'

In an editorial in *Liberator*, the newspaper of the Young Liberal movement, that appeared in July/August 1975, proportional representation was attacked on the grounds that (a) 'it looks like becoming a tool for reactionary centrist government' — a point answered above — and (b) 'it is essentially peripheral to the need to vest power with the people'. The article continues: 'Making Parliament more representative will still not alter the fact that power does not lie in parliamentary government but rather with capitalists, technocrats and bureaucrats. It could be another con on an electorate increasingly disillusioned with the charade of parliamentary politics and looking for a radical alternative.'

There are two possible responses to this. One is that the 'radical alternative' may have its attractions for people who favour the idea of small self-governing or 'participatory' units of authority. These could be schools, hospitals, companies, local councils, or whatever — the only comment necessary here is that such units will eventually want managing committees if they are to be efficient. Those committees will be more representative, and the self-governing units more participatory if the super-vote is used to elect them.

The second response is that while we have large modern industrial states there will be power at the centre. This power may be military or dictatorial — but if it professes to be democratic then the more strength that is given to elected representative institutions that can control the executive authority, the better. Capitalists, technocrats, and bureaucrats (and it should be added trade union leaders) will always attempt to influence or control this central power. They will have far less chance of success if they are dealing with a truly representative and revitalised Parliament.

Which system — the double vote or the super-vote?

To provide the opportunity for British voters to elect such a Parliament militant democrats must work for a change to a fairer voting system. But which one?

The primary, to choose candidates, would at best help to solve only one of the problems facing our democracy — the tendency for small factions to win control over the selection of party candidates. Addressing the Labour Party at Blackpool on 30 September 1975 Mr Harold Wilson described this particular problem as 'a take-over bid for a 20,000-majority seat based on an incursion of little more than a dozen people'.

If all candidates were chosen by a statutory ballot of party members before the vote then a take-over bid would require a few hundred, or a few thousand, supporters if it was to be successful — the exact number would depend on how many people turned out to vote in the primary (Chapter 5).

Mr Wilson put the danger another way: 'Can anyone in a broad democratic movement such as ours assert the claim that a man or woman elected by 25,000 Labour voters one week should be given his cards the following week by a small group of fifty, who in themselves represent only one in 500 of the Labour voters who elected him and who only last year recommended him to the electorate.

This kind of thing could be avoided by a simple party rule that an MP can only be dismissed following a postal ballot of all the local members of his or her party. Like primaries, such a rule may help prevent undemocratic take-overs by tiny groups although neither device would be a complete safeguard. Nor would primaries or postal ballots do much else to make our system more democratic beyond giving members of a party (not the same thing as the voters as a whole) some say over which individual or candidate should represent it.

The second vote or the alternative vote can be as unfair and divisive as the system it is intended to replace. A straight party list system would probably be rejected by most people in this country. These can all be passed over.

We are left with a choice between the system used in Ireland (the super-vote) and the one used in West Germany (the double vote).

Each has special merits; each has particular disadvantages. The super-vote as used in Ireland is too restrictive, with too many three- and four-member constituencies. We would have to divide the country in such a way that the average constituency size was about five. This would mean fair representation for at least 84 per cent of the voters. Those who recoil from the idea of five-member constituencies might think about Churchill's comment that he would rather be one-fifth of the representative for the whole of Leeds than the whole representative for one-fifth of Leeds.

Some British psephologists have calculated that if we had five-member maxi-constituencies the results would be on the pattern of two Conservative, two Labour, one Liberal in many or most of them. The comment is usually added that such a distribution would be inequitable, because the first-preference votes would not always divide in such a neat proportion.

A study of what has happened in Ireland over the past half-century should put such people's minds at rest. Even with their three- and four-member constituencies the share of seats won by the leading parties is usually remarkably close to the division of first-preference votes. There is a built-in bias against smaller parties, but this is true of any realistic system of proportional representation, since the alternative is the very fragmentation of which opponents of all such systems make so much.

The calculation that British five-member constituencies would frequently return MPs on a 2-2-1 pattern ignores later preferences. It leaves the nationalist parties out of account. And it makes the fundamental error of assuming that you can tell exactly how people will vote in a super-vote election by studying X-vote results.

It must be said against the super-vote that if there is a campaign to use it for British Parliamentary elections its opponents may be able to make some headway by complaining that it is complicated, and perhaps more headway by playing on a possible misunderstanding of how multi-member constituencies would work.

Yet it may be possible to convince people that the super-vote has the most powerful claim of them all to give the individual voter personal representation. It is better than any other at allowing a choice between candidates and factions within parties. Of all systems it is the most proof against 'tactical voting' — voting in one direction in order to give a contrary result. With the West German double vote you can support an alliance by voting for one partner with the constituency first vote and another with the party-list second vote.

In short, the super-vote could be the fairest way of giving the most power over Parliament to the largest number of people.

The double vote may be easier to campaign for because half the seats are filled by MPs representing single-member constituencies. To achieve this in Britain it would be necessary to double the size of existing constituencies, so that the number of MPs could remain the same as it is now — half elected in constituencies, and half through the party lists. The alternative would be increasing the size of Parliament to 800 or 900 members, or possibly even doubling it.

The counting system is not particularly easy to explain, but most people should find that they can quickly grasp its purpose as fair shares of seats in Parliament. This may be easier to put across than the transfer of choices involved in the more sophisticated super-vote.

The West German system is, for parties, the more perfectly proportional of the two. Its barrier against small parties keeps it from being fissiparous. Yet when the detailed arithmetic is studied, and the results of experience of these systems in use are remembered, it is seen that with either of them there would be room for all parties as large as all the national and nationalist parties presently represented at Westminster; in both cases small fringe parties would still be kept out. This would still be true even if our rules were slightly more liberal than the Irish or the West German rules.

The existence of constituency members in the double vote system may be pleasing to our own traditionalists. But the representative of a single seat in a five-member super-vote constituency is likely to be more closely tied to the people than either the run-of-the-mill British MP in a middling to safe seat, or a West German MP. With the super-vote no seat is ever really safe. The MP must always fight, at every election, for first-preference votes. The West German MP can have an arrangement made to put him high on the party list if he loses favour in his own constituency.

With the super-vote you would not need primaries; the primary is built into its mechanism. There can be any number of candidates and voters can choose 1,2,3,4 ... without risking the loss of their party's fair share of seats. The West German method gives as much effective power to the party machine as does the British X-vote. It would be essential to introduce some kind of statutory primary vote to keep the selection of candidates out of the hands of party committees; with that the double vote might be closer to the British ideal (never realised) of a reasonable balance between the power of party machines and the power of ordinary people.

In a perfect world the super-vote would be the best choice. The trouble is that the question, 'Which is the best system?' must be modified by the more difficult question, 'Which is the likeliest to be accepted?' Until he or she can be certain of the answer to this the cunning democrat will persistently argue the case for the single transferable vote — while leaving open the option of coming out strongly for the double vote, if at the end of the day it looks like a more certain winner. The same applies, the other way round, to those who may start off with a preference for the double vote. What is essential is to avoid so splitting the campaign for electoral reform that it destroys itself.

After all, the difference that choosing one or other of these two possible systems would make would be marginal compared with the difference that would be made by a change from what we now have to any system of proportional representation at all.

How can Parliament be captured?
Our major political parties will not agree to any such change unless they are forced to. Each prefers to live in hopes of another unfettered spell of office; neither likes to contemplate the necessity of truly democratic representation. The question, therefore, boils down to: what is likely to force a change?

An election result in which no single party won an overall majority might do it. The Liberals would probably demand electoral reform as a price for participating in such a forced coalition — although no one can guarantee that it would be the Liberals who would hold the balance of power.

The unravelling might begin in Scotland. The Scottish Nationalists might hold the balance of power in a future British Parliament if they continue to advance as far in future years as they did between the elections of 1970 and 1974. They could displace Labour as the holder of more than half of Scotland's seventy-one seats. To do this they would need to increase their share of the Scottish vote from the 30 per cent achieved in October 1974 to somewhere nearer to 40 per cent. This is quite possible, given their record. If they did so the resulting chaos at Westminster might provide an opportunity for those who favour electoral reform to press their case.

Or it could be that the new Scottish Assembly, if there is one, is granted the super-vote. Westminster politicians might do this for the bad reason that they wanted to prevent the Scottish Nationalists from gaining overall control of the assembly (something that could not be prevented with proportional representation if the Scottish National Party won more than half the votes). If Northern Ireland, Scotland, and Wales all had super-vote-elected assemblies it would be that much harder to deny the same fair voting system to the whole country.

Opinion polls in both spring 1974 and autumn 1975 suggest that once confronted with the facts about Britain's present voting system most people agree that there should be a change to something fairer. It is not impossible that a national campaign to win mass support for electoral reform might succeed. The hope may be forlorn, but it exists. Many millions of people are looking for a new direction, a new sense of purpose for British political life: the polls, and the evidence of our senses, tell us that. Fair voting could never be the whole answer, but it could be the first motto on the first banner in a march that could become long and crowded. Those who do not despair, those who have hope for Britain, should work to raise that first banner high.

Acknowledgements
Bibliography

Acknowledgements

The detailed suggestions for corrections and improvements made by Miss Enid Lakeman were invaluable. Mr James Knight was especially helpful with Chapter 10, as was Professor Richard Rose with Chapter 11. The polling organisations, Gallup, NOP Market Research Ltd, and Opinion Research Centre, a member of the Louis Harris International Group, were most forthcoming. I am also indebted for assistance to Mr Ben Patterson, of the European Parliament Information Centre, my father, Nelson Rogaly, Mr Ian Davidson, Mr Rex Winsbury, Mrs Anneliese Bingham, and my long-suffering family.

Bibliography

W. Bagehot, *The English Constitution*, Chapman & Hall, 1867.

S. Brittan, *Left or Right, The Bogus Dilemma*, Secker & Warburg, 1968.

J.M. Burns, and J.W. Peltason, *Government by the People*, Prentice-Hall, 1963.

D.E. Butler, *The Electoral System in Britain, 1918-1951*, Clarendon Press, Oxford, 1953.

D.E. Butler, *The British General Election of 1955*, Macmillan, 1955.

D.E. Butler, and J. Freeman, *British Political Facts, 1900-1960*, Macmillan, 1963.

D.E. Butler and D. Kavanagh, *The British General Election of February 1974*, Macmillan, 1974.

D.E. Butler, and D. Stokes, *Political Change in Britain*, Macmillan, 1974.

B. Chubb, 'Going about Persecuting Civil Servants', *Political Studies*, vol. II, 1963, pp.272-286.

S.E. Finer, ed., *Adversary Politics and Electoral Reform*, collected essays, Anthony Wigram, 1975.

A. Giddens, *The Class Structure of the Advanced Societies*, Hutchinson, 1973.

P. Hain, *Radical Regeneration*, Anchor Press, 1975.

F.A. Hermens, *The Representative Republic*, University of Notre Dame Press, 1958.

U.W. Kitzinger, *German Electoral Politics*, Clarendon Press, Oxford, 1960.

J. Knight, and N. Baxter-Moore, *Northern Ireland. The Elections of the Twenties*, Arthur McDougall Fund, London 1972.

J. Knight, and N. Baxter-Moore, *The Republic of Ireland. The General Elections of 1969 & 1973*, Arthur McDougall Fund, 1973.

J. Knight, *Northern Ireland. The Elections of 1973*, Arthur McDougall Fund, 1974.

J. Knight, *Northern Ireland. The Election of the Constitutional Convention*, Arthur McDougall Fund, 1975.

E. Lakeman, *How Democracies Vote — A Study of Electoral Systems*, Faber, 1974.

R.L. Leonard, *Elections in Britain*, D. Van Nostrand, 1968.

W.J.M. Mackenzie, *Free Elections*, Allen & Unwin, 1958.

T.H. Mackie and R. Rose, *The International Almanac of Electoral History*, Macmillan Press, 1974.

J.L. McCracken, *Representative Government in Ireland*, Oxford University Press, 1958.

J.S. Mill, *On Liberty. Considerations On Representative Government*, Basil Blackwell, 1946.

C.A. Moser, *Survey Methods in Social Investigation*, Heinemann, 1958.
Parliamentary Reform, The Hansard Society, Cassell, 1967.
D. Pickles, *The Fifth French Republic*, Methuen, 1965.
R. Rose, ed., *Electoral Behaviour. A Comparative Handbook*, Collier Macmillan, 1974.
J.F.S. Ross, *Elections and Electors. Studies in democratic representation*, Eyre & Spottiswoode, 1955.
J.F.S. Ross, *The Irish Election System. What it is and How it works*, Pall Mall Press, 1959.
J.A. Schumpeter, *Capitalism, Socialism & Democracy*, Allen & Unwin, 1970.

OFFICIAL REPORTS AND PAMPHLETS

J. Arnold, *Democracy for Europe, Direct Elections to the European Parliament. The Possibilities*, Bow Group, 1975.
Sir William Beveridge, *Social Insurance & Allied Services*, Report, HMSO, 1958 (Cmd 6404).
N. Clarke, *The Story of the Great Vote Robbery*, Liberal Action Group for Electoral Reform, 1975.
W.W. Daniel, *The PEP Survey on Inflation*, vol. XLI, Broadsheet 553, PEP, 1975.
Democracy and Devolution Proposals for Scotland and Wales, HMSO, 1974, (Cmd. 5732).
Devolution within the United Kingdom, Some Alternatives for Discussion, HMSO, 1974.
A.D.R. Dickson, 'When Rejects Re-Run. A Study in Independency', *Political Quarterly*, vol. 46, 3, July-Aug. 1975, p.271.
H. Finer, *Fabian Tract 211*, Fabian Society, 1924.
J. Gilmour and J. Woodward-Nutt, *Electing the Scottish Assembly*, Electoral Reform Society, 1975.
Harris Polls and the General Election on 28 February 1974, section 4, 'Apologia to Daily Express Readers', pp. 10-12, Louis Harris International Inc., 1974.
The Labour Party, *Report of the Twenty-Sixth Annual Conference*, *Labour's Programme for Britain*, Annual Conference 1973, Labour Party, 1973.
E. Lakeman, *Nine Democracies (Electoral Systems of the Countries of the EEC)*, Arthur McDougall Fund, 1975.
N. Lamont MP, *Electoral Reform, No Reform*, Bow Group, 1975.
A Language for Life, Report of the Committee of Inquiry, appointed by the Secretary of State for Education & Science, under the Chairmanship of Sir Alan Bullock, HMSO, 1975.
New Outlook, vol. 15, 7, July 1975, 'On Devolution, Nationalism, Electoral Reform'.
M. Nissel, ed., *Social Trends 5*, HMSO, 1974.
NOP Political Bulletins, especially February 1975, 133, p. 26. National Opinion Polls Ltd., 1975.

Northern Ireland, Constitutional Proposals, HMSO, 1973, (Cmd 5259).
Northern Ireland, Discussion Paper 2: 'Constitutional Convention Procedure', HMSO, 1974.
Northern Ireland, Statutory Instruments 1973, 890, 'The Northern Ireland Assembly (Election) Order 1973', HMSO, 1973.
R. Rose, *The Future of Scottish Politics,* The Fraser of Allander Institute Speculative Papers 3, Scottish Academic Press, Edinburgh, 1975.
Royal Commission on the Constitution, 1969-73, vol. I, Report, HMSO, 1973 (Cmd 5460).
Royal Commission on the Constitution, 1969-73, vol. II, Memorandum of Dissent by Lord Crowther-Hunt and Prof. A.T. Peacock, HMSO 1973 (Cmd 5460).
Royal Commission on the Distribution of Income & Wealth, Report I, Initial Report on the Standing Reference, HMSO, 1975 (Cmd 6171).

USEFUL ADDRESSES

The Hansard Society for Parliamentary Government,
12 Gower Street, London, WC1E 6DP.

Conservative Action for Electoral Reform (CAER),
6 Queen Street, Mayfair, London W1

Electoral Reform Society,
6 Chancel Street, Southwark, London SE1 OUX

Liberal Action Group for Electoral Reform (LAGER)
1a Whitehall Place, London SW1